"In her new book, *Choose to Believe*, Paige Lee delivers life experiences woven together by strength and courage. Her world would forever be changed, but we discover that miracles, healing, and the afterlife inspired and encouraged her to see beyond loss. One mother's heart-wrenching story of loss and maternal love will move you: body, mind, and spirit. Paige teaches how to awaken a new understanding of living beyond the loss, seeing the signs from beyond, and finding joy on your journey through grief."

– ROLAND COMTOIS, Medium, Speaker, and
Author of *Signs of Spirit*

"Paige Lee has written a must-read account of a mother's love and of saying good-bye too soon, inviting us all to trust in eternal life, continued connection with lost loved ones and a closer relationship to Spirit... Read this book and deepen your faith in love, God and maybe even yourself."

– JILL RENEE FEELER, Visionary in cosmology,
consciousness and spirituality

"*Choose to Believe* is a perfect example of the uplifting energy that Paige exudes to all those around her. Through this work, she has proven that love lives forever and that our loved ones in spirit are still right here, cheering us on and encouraging us to move forward into a more positive, purpose-driven life, knowing that each breath we take guides us closer to our children in spirit. I know that Bryan is very proud of his mama!"

– ELIZABETH BOISSON, President and Co-Founder,
Helping Parents Heal, Inc.

"The tragic murder of her son, Bryan, was the catalyst for Paige Lee's cathartic journey that led to her transformation. Opening her heart and mind to possibilities she'd not previously considered, Paige came to see a blurring of the lines between life and death. Was Bryan still alive in some form and able to confirm his well-being? It seemed so, and that made all the difference as Paige experienced healing and discovered a renewed sense of life purpose."

– MARK IRELAND, Author of
Soul Shift: Finding Where the Dead Go
and *Messages from the Afterlife*

"As a bereaved mother and spirit medium, Paige's story resonates with my own experiences and knowing. I applaud Paige for diving into the depths of her healing and authentically sharing with her readers what she has learned. Paige found her son, Bryan, and she also found deep healing and empowerment that comes from getting to know one's own soul and higher power. I highly recommend *Choose To Believe* to any grieving person who is in search of healing."

– RACHEL PEARSON, Spirit Medium and author of *Start It Up*

"As we are brought into this mother's grief and the experiences that follow, it is one of beautiful unconditional love and excruciating pain, one of undeniable growth and wondrous awareness. Paige Lee takes us moment to moment through what many bereaved parents face without warning, preparation, or resources. The death of her child. She also realizes as she travels this unknown path there is a bigger story unfolding. One of connection and hope, of reaching out for support and trusting a journey she could never have imagined. *Choose To Believe* is for us and others to grasp the reality of life and death, to witness through this mom's raw, yet eloquent words how her love only grew for her beloved only child. As a mom who has grieved the loss of my only child as well, I know *Choose to Believe* will bring many insights and healing components to her readers. This truly is a love story…"

– SARA RUBLE, Scott's mom, *Spiritteaches.org*

Choose
to BELIEVE

A Story of Miracles, Healing,
and the Afterlife

Choose
to BELIEVE

A Story of Miracles, Healing,
and the Afterlife

by

Paige W. Lee

Ladybug Media
Eagle, Idaho USA

Cover by Terry Hansen

Ladybug Media • Eagle, Idaho USA

Dedication page poem, reprinted by permission of
Vironika Tugaleva

ISBN:
978-1-7355699-0-1

Library of Congress Control Number:
2020915348

To Dwaine

You are the rock that roots my fire.
You are the Earth that grounds my soul.
                              - Vironika Tugaleva

To Tayler, Ryenn, Hadley, Maddyn, and Everett

If I can stop one heart from breaking,
I shall not live in vain;
If I can ease one life the aching,
Or cool one pain,
Or help one fainting robin
Unto his nest again,
I shall not live in vain.
                              - Emily Dickinson

Table of Contents

Number 1 Bestselling author of
Permission to Mourn and *Becoming Radiant*

"When I heal, you heal. When you heal, I heal.
We're all connected."

I do believe that healing is possible. I don't, however, believe that healing is always a destination. Sometimes, at least for me, healing becomes my way of being in the world. My intention is to consciously heal a little more every day. Intention. Vision. Action. I'm okay with that.

In her own personal love letter to life itself, *Choose to Believe*, my friend Paige Lee, Bryan's always and forever mom, has painted a picture for you. A picture of what healing can look, feel, taste, sound and smell like for you. Yes, for you.

Intimately, vulnerably and honestly Paige shares her life with us. She shares her son Bryan's death with us. And the aftermath. The aftermath. And most importantly Paige shares the concrete, measurable, doable action steps she took (and continues to take) over and over and over again on her road to healing. Paige made the decision that she not only wanted to heal, but that she was going to co-create her healing. With her God. With her son Bryan. With life itself. Paige made the bold and courageous decision that yes, a mother whose "son Bryan was killed in a senseless act of murder in 2008, at the tender age of twenty-three" could actually heal. Still, a revolutionary and upsetting-to-some concept in 2020. Healing is possible. There is a new way. A new way to do grief which creates a new way to do life. Paige is living life in a new way.

Paige Lee has experienced the indescribable pain and horror of the death of a beloved. Step-by-step-by-step Paige has consciously created her own radiant resurrection. Her powerful book *Choose to Believe* tells that story in a way that you can make it your story. Paige generously shares her knowledge, her wisdom and the tools she gathered along the way so that you, too, can become radiant. If you are interested in healing your shattered heart following the death of your beloved, this is a must read. A must read! Let the healing begin!

Thank you Paige for shining your light,

With love,

Tom Zuba

LETTER TO MY READERS

I am honored that you have found your way to this book. As nothing ever happens by coincidence, I trust that you have been led here for a reason. I want you to know how deeply sorry I am for the pain you have in your heart. I know that pain; I have known it again and again throughout my life. But nothing ever compared or ever will compare to the pain I felt after my son Bryan was killed in a senseless act of murder in 2008, at the tender age of twenty-three. His death catapulted me on a journey that has been equally heart-wrenching, soul-breaking, uplifting, confusing, enlightening, and transformative.

Throughout the twists and turns that I have taken on my grief-healing journey, I have learned that my son still lives, and that I can still have a relationship with him. We walk together now, side by side. We strive to help other people, especially parents, understand that their relationships with their children don't have to end just because their children have died. We share the greater reality that only the body ever dies. Our loved ones' souls live eternally, just as their love for us is infinite and never ending.

Your grief-healing journey will be unique to you—it probably won't look exactly like mine. But I have found that there are so many similarities in each person's journey that it seems important to present my path to you. Maybe, just maybe, this book can help you see that

a) you aren't crazy;
b) you aren't alone;
c) your connections to your loved ones are within you, and that is where you can ultimately choose to find them: within you.

As a self-defined Seeker, I pursued many different workshops and accredited programs throughout my own searching, but it doesn't require classes or certifications or large amounts of money to find your 'lost' loved one (spoiler alert: they aren't lost at all). I will introduce you to the tools and the people who helped me along the way, reveal to you the findings that my searching brought me, and explain which ones ultimately became my truth, for they may resonate with you as well.

Above all else, though, I write this book to give you hope. To show you that you can survive what may be the biggest tragedy of your lifetime. Not only can you survive it, but you can even enjoy a wonderful, loving and joyous life. I want to honor the commitment I made to myself and to my son to tell our story and make it available for those who may be helped by it. I want my grandkids to know Bryan through me. I hope you will feel like you know him just a little bit, as well. He really was, and still is, an absolutely incredible spirit. I am so very lucky to be his mom and to have had him with us on this earth for twenty-three wonderful, amazing, joy-filled years.

I have been blessed with so much insight, so many friendships, so much peace as I have navigated this journey through my grief. And also, so much growth. My prayer for you is that you will have similar blessings on your own journey. With deep respect for you and your story, from my heart to yours, I humbly send you love, peace and gratitude.

Paige

CHAPTER ONE
The Dream

It was a late August night in 2008. As I slept, I gazed up at my beloved grandmother's angelic presence. She was seated in a chair that was mostly concealed by her draping white gown, her beautiful long, silver gray hair falling across her shoulders and down her back. I was seated at her feet. She whispered to me softly, "It's okay darling, you will be with us soon." That was all. Those were the only words I remembered from my dream that night. I later came to understand that my grandmother had come to me in a dream visit—this was no ordinary dream. A dream visit is literally a visit from a deceased person, from God or an angelic being, during our sleep time. For me, the difference between a dream visit and a regular dream is the absolute vividness of the dream visit and how it becomes permanently embedded in my memory with precise details that do not fade over time. Dream visits can sometimes contain warnings, news, or other important information, but our loved ones will always be loving in a visit, they will never appear menacing, angry, disappointed, or depressed.

I took Grandma's words literally. "You will be with us soon" surely meant that my time was up. The big guy upstairs was calling my number. I began to get my affairs in order—made sure our wills were up to date and accessible, made a list of personal property items I wanted to gift to specific individuals, made sure our bookkeeping was current, made a list of passwords for my husband to be able to have access to everything he would need, told some loved ones where certain special items could be found. You know the drill; I thought I was going to die. I prepared to leave this earthly world.

Little did I know then, that my entire world was going to fall out from underneath me. Little did I know, then, that I wasn't the one who was going to die.

CHAPTER TWO

The Death

My son and only living birth child, Bryan Richard Frost, was twenty-three years young and in his final semester at the University of Southern California's prestigious School of Cinematic Arts. Film school! Bryan had been back in Los Angeles for about three weeks following the summer break, during which he had spent three and a half months in Pakistan visiting his friend from Karachi. Together they were filming "Karbala," a fictional story that Bryan wrote about an Iraqi police chief who secretly leads an ambush against American soldiers. Bryan and his friend were very excited about the film, and they worked tirelessly in 120-plus degree heat to get as much of the filming done as they could. Bryan was supposed to come home for two weeks between leaving Pakistan and returning to school, but at the tail end of his trip he decided to take a well-deserved break and travel to Northern Pakistan to explore the

Himalayan Mountain region. He wasn't sure he would make it home at all before heading back to school, he explained when he called to tell me his plans, but I begged him to please come home. So, he did. Bryan came home on August 17, 2008 for eight days— eight short days that I had to share with his father and his friends. But we were able to spend a great deal of time together, for which I was grateful. Bryan was a changed young man when he returned from Pakistan. He was calmer, and he had a quiet assurance and passion about him. I was excited for his future and the experiences he had been able to have over the summer.

On August 25, 2008 I said good-bye to Bryan at the airport and watched him make his way through security and toward his gate. He went back to Los Angeles to prepare for his final semester of school.

Bryan called me in the mid-evening hours of September 17, 2008. Oh, how I loved it when he called me. "Hi Mom," he said. "How's it going?" We talked about his new apartment. He was disappointed because the living room was about as big as a closet, and the third bedroom was barely larger than that. He had already decided, though, to convince his two roommates to let him pay less than one-third of the rent if he volunteered to take the small room. That's my Bryan—always the negotiator. At one point in our conversation I told him I hadn't been feeling well all day, and would it be all right if I called him back tomorrow. But, thankfully, we just kept on talking and didn't hang up right away. I asked what he was planning to do that night and he said he would probably go out for a beer later. I remember so clearly, urging him, "Don't go out tonight Bryan, it's too late. Stay home and watch a movie or something." He told me he'd been calling around and had found a guy that had agreed to go with him—they were only going out for a couple of beers. We ended the call like we always did, with "I Love You."

September 18, 2008

I had always said that the day I had to leave my son at West Point Military Academy was the worst day of my life. Until September 18, 2008, which would forever become the worst day of my life.

I was awakened by a phone call shortly after 5:00 a.m. from one of Bryan's roommates. Someone had called him and said Bryan had been in a fight and had been taken to the hospital. The roommate was there, at California Medical Center, but no one would tell him anything about Bryan's condition. He told me he thought Bryan was okay but no one would talk to him and asked if I would please call the hospital and then let him know what was going on. Instantly awake, I called the hospital only to meet with frustrating roadblocks. Because of privacy laws, no one would tell me anything about my son; they wouldn't even confirm that he had been admitted. For at least an hour I didn't know anything, worry building up like a volcano inside of me. Then my phone rang again. It was Michael Jackson, then Vice-president of Student Affairs at

USC. I was confused as to why he would be calling but begged him to tell me what was happening—I knew only that Bryan had been taken to the hospital.

I will never, ever forget his next words, his voice. "So, you know your son has passed away."

And that is how my nightmare began.

The next couple of weeks are a hazy blur. It's kind of funny, what you remember. I don't remember my husband, Dwaine, coming into the room and picking my phone up off the floor, but I remember packing to go to L.A. to bring my son home. I was so worried about what to take—in the end I packed half-outfits and not enough of anything. I don't remember Dwaine calling my best friend, Lynn, but I remember she showed up out of nowhere. I imagine he also had the horrible task of notifying our other two children, my stepkids, Jade and Steven, both of whom were very close to Bryan, and Bryan's stepsister from my previous marriage, Whitney, who had remained close to our family and especially to Bryan. I vaguely remember calling Bryan's dad, Jere, and just crying on the phone.

The next thing I knew I was at the airport. Someone, I'm not sure who, made the travel arrangements for us. I think it was Bryan's stepmother, Danetta. She and Jere were waiting for us at the airport, along with Jere's parents, sister and brother-in-law. I ran up to my ex-husband and hugged him, sobbing and crying out,

"We shouldn't have let him go to L.A.; we shouldn't have let him go to L.A." He just hugged me and said, "There's nothing we could have done, Paige."

You see, when the time had come for Bryan to make a decision about college, he wanted nothing less than the best education he could possibly get. In part because we couldn't afford to send him to an Ivy League school, he chose to apply for a military academy appointment. He decided that the opportunity to receive such a high-level education AND serve his country was the best of all worlds. Bryan didn't just receive one academy appointment—he received three appointments to West Point, two to the Air Force Academy and one to the Naval Academy. Such is the way it always was with our over-achieving child. He chose West Point, and off he went on a new adventure.

I remember that first summer when Bryan was in boot camp. He would write us letters almost every day and I would sit on my back deck and write him letters every morning. Bryan was a gifted writer, and his letters were so descriptive that I almost felt I was there with him. It was a very hard summer and many boys quit, but Bryan toughed it out. He was never a quitter at anything he did. He didn't cheat or take the easy way out, ever. He stayed at West Point for a year and a half, but with time he realized that the military life was not what he was looking for. So he had the courage to leave the academy, even though doing so may have disappointed some people that he loved and respected. Of course, while he was there he made the academic Dean's List every semester.

Because Bryan left West Point mid-year, he wasn't eligible to transfer to many universities until the beginning of the next school year. Many kids would have taken the semester off to regroup, chill, and hang out with their friends back home. Not Bryan. He didn't want to waste a whole semester, so he transferred to a school in Colorado that did allow mid-year transfers. While there, he applied to USC and was accepted as an Economics major. His father and I struggled with the tuition but agreed to pay for it, with the help of Bryan's scholarships, because we knew how much it meant to our son. Bryan was SO excited to become a Trojan. He finished his economics degree and then chose to pursue a second degree after discovering a love and passion for filmmaking.

So even though I knew that Bryan traveled the path he wanted to travel, perhaps was destined to travel, I wanted to blame myself. *We shouldn't have let him go to Los Angeles. We should have refused to pay for it, then he would have stayed home, or in Colorado--anywhere that wasn't Los Angeles!* Truthfully, I never liked Bryan's being there. We live in Eagle, Idaho, part of the greater Boise area, where there is very little crime. I would constantly tell Bryan to be careful, to not stray beyond the "safe" areas of campus, to be alert and watchful. He always assured me that, while there were some unsafe neighborhoods in proximity to USC, the campus and housing areas were safe and told me not to worry. I can't tell you how many times we had that conversation. And until that fateful night, he was safe.

Guilt grabbed hold of me and wouldn't let me go. It was

unforgiving, unrelenting. *How is it that I wasn't there to protect my son? Why didn't I know he was in trouble last night? How could I not have known?* (Ah, but did I know? Is that why I didn't want him to go out that evening, practically begged him not to?)

I don't remember the flight to Los Angeles at all, other than just staring blindly out the window, quietly crying. I remember that because my husband always prefers to have the window seat, but he offered it to me this time. We were greeted at LAX by Bryan's friends and roommates and some representatives from USC. I remember feeling so sorry for them, that they had to deal with us. How do you console grieving parents? You can't. With compassion, they said the obligatory condolences and gathered our luggage for us. Then they whisked us into a car and took us to USC.

I would swear that every person we walked by as we made our way to the president's office knew who we were and why we were there. I just knew they were whispering to each other, "Look . . . those are the parents of the guy who was killed this morning." I wondered if any of them knew Bryan, wondered if they were mourning him as we were. We met with the vice-president of Student Affairs and the president of USC, who told us how wonderful our son was and what a great contribution he had made to the student body and to the school. *GET ME OUT OF HERE* was all I could think to myself, as I politely nodded my head when it was appropriate, tried to smile when it seemed like they wanted me to, and dried my tears so that I wouldn't fall apart in front of these strangers. I know they had good intentions but quite honestly, I could have done without talking to these people in the first twenty-four hours following my son's death.

Up until then we didn't know very much about the details of Bryan's death. We knew he had been in a fight and that the other person had stabbed Bryan, and that Bryan had died. That was all.

Thankfully, USC had made arrangements for the two Los Angeles Police Department homicide detectives who were handling the case to meet with us. They told us everything. I will tell you the short version of the story, as objectively as I can, and without prejudice.

After calling many of his friends to go out that evening, Bryan had found someone who said yes. That person brought one of his friends along. The three of them met at a local tavern just a few blocks away from campus. All three of the boys lived on or just off campus. (Bryan's apartment was about two blocks north of campus.) Each of the three boys had a few drinks. They left the bar around 2:00 a.m. and headed toward a friend's house. As only fate would have it, they missed the street they were supposed to turn on and found themselves needing to backtrack a bit. As they were heading back to the correct street, they passed an apartment building. This apartment building had a wrought-iron fence and gate along the front of the property. The gate was standing wide open and Bryan reached over and slammed it shut. Just moments before, a car had arrived at the apartment building. A man about the same age as my son ran from that parked car, yelling and wanting to know who was slamming his gate. The man swung at Bryan, and Bryan fought back. They grappled to the ground and Bryan ended up pinning the man, sitting on his chest. After a moment, Bryan got up, let the man walk away, and rejoined his friends at the street corner. The man's girlfriend got out of the driver's seat of the car and yelled at the boys, shouting obscenities, presumably to detain them. Then the man came running back out of the apartment building, toward Bryan. Bryan started walking toward him and said, "Hey man, what's up? Just let us go," or something along those lines. The man ran up to Bryan, laid a final blow to Bryan's chest, ran to his girlfriend's car, and they raced off. The boys were crossing the street to leave when Bryan grabbed his chest, saw blood, and said, "Oh man, I think I've been stabbed." He then collapsed on the street. His friends called 911. The ambulance arrived very quickly and took Bryan to the hospital, but it was too late. (We later found out that Bryan died in the ambulance with only the paramedic by his side.)

The detectives told us they didn't know who Bryan's murderer was, but they had some leads. They promised us they would find him. And they did, after a few agonizing weeks. He is now serving a twenty-five-to-life sentence for second degree murder. The prosecutor couldn't quite prove premeditation to the jury, so they were unable to convict on first degree.

We were in L.A. for a total of four days. USC gave us a car and driver while we were there. During that time, we went to the hospital to talk to the doctor who was on call when Bryan was brought in. I wanted to know what Bryan's condition was when he arrived there, did he say anything, did he ask for me? (We didn't know at that point that he had died in the ambulance.) As soon as we walked into the hospital, I had a panic attack and couldn't control my emotions. The instant we walked through the door I was completely overwhelmed with sadness and regret that I wasn't there to hold Bryan's hand when he needed me. I was sick with the thought that he had died in that ugly place with no one nearby who loved him. To think that those gray walls may have been the last thing he saw . . .

I will never forget the security guard who was on duty, and how nice he was to me. We were told the doctor was not in that day, so instead he took us down to the records department so we could fill out the required paperwork to get Bryan's medical records. They promised they would send them to us. To this day, I haven't seen them. I think Bryan's father might have them. Ironically, when I was back in Los Angeles ten months later for the trial of my son's murderer, I ended up having acute bronchitis from stress, and my sister-in-law took me to the closest hospital. As soon as I walked in the door, I knew I was in the same hallway, the same hospital, the same place where my son had died, and I experienced another violent panic attack. Lo and behold, the very same security guard came to my aid, and it wasn't long before he and the attending nurse made the connection as to who I was. "USC," they said—no further explanation was necessary.

The one bright spot of this entire trip was that we got to meet

Bryan's core group of friends while we were there. Bryan had many, many friends, but these eight kids in particular are special; they are truly amazing. They come from all corners of the world, from different religions and different cultures. Yet these friends were so close, so connected to each other, so committed to being the best friend they could be for each other. When Bryan died, they came together as a group and spent as much time with us as they could. Clearly, they needed us as much as we needed them. They all piled into two cars and made the nineteen-hour drive to Boise for the funeral. Two months later, they came back for Thanksgiving and then they came AGAIN the following February over Presidents Day weekend. Five months after that, four of them visited us during the Fourth of July weekend. My husband and I—and everyone we know—we've never seen anything like it. Just by wanting to be with us and be a part of Bryan's family, those kids did more for our initial healing than anyone else could have done. I love them all dearly. They called Boise "Home Base," and I know we will see them again.

I don't remember exactly everything that we did while we were in L.A. I don't remember going to bed at night, but I do remember waking up early in the morning and going into the bathroom to cry. I didn't want Dwaine to hear my pain; it was too private and raw even to share with my husband. The first morning, I sat in that hotel bathroom and I was in such a state of shock, still. I stared at myself in the mirror, tears streaming down my face, and I wondered *Who am I? I can't be me—this can't be happening to me.* Bryan was my life's blood, the person I was closest to, my best buddy, and sometimes the biggest pain in my butt, but always he was my one and only child. My son. From the day he was born, everything I worked for and everything I did was for him.

We were waiting for the medical examiner to release our son's body so we could take him home with us. Although we had been told it wasn't necessary, we asked to be driven to the coroner's office. I remember the long, sad drive to the coroner's office as if it just happened yesterday. The reality of that place is as cold and uninviting as you would imagine. We were led into a small room and asked to wait; I remember feeling a bit like a caged animal inside that small room with four bare walls and a door leading into what we presumed was the morgue. My heart was pounding, I was terrified of what the next few moments would bring. The four of us were silent as we waited. Finally, the door opened, and the coroner walked in. After agreeing to expedite the autopsy, he explained that he needed someone to make a positive ID. Because Bryan had been in a fight, he told us that it wasn't "very pretty" and recommended we make a photo identification versus a physical one.

That's when I lost it again. What in God's name are we doing here? What has happened? Is this even real? *WAKE UP! BRYAN, WHERE ARE YOU?* Needless to say, I couldn't bring myself to look at the picture. Bryan's father made the ID.

Then we had to go to Bryan's apartment and pack up his things. It was so sad to see how few things my son actually possessed. He always got by with very little and never asked for much. For a long time, I sat on his bed and cried, while Jere and Dwaine went to get boxes and tape. Danetta and I started going through everything, packing up every little thing that brought back a memory of Bryan. Bryan when he was alive, just like you and me. Framed photographs, his lacrosse stick, his snowboard, all of his writings and film scripts, his camera, his tapes of the film shorts he had made in school, notes he had taken during a long phone conversation we'd had, the budget I had created with him the previous spring, the cookbooks he asked me to buy for him, his computer—it was surreal, actually. To be in Bryan's room, in an apartment that we had never seen before, going through his things—I felt like an intruder. Like the mom I never was—the one who goes through her kid's room to see if she can find drugs or Playboy magazines. As I sat on his bed sorting through his things, there was so much that I recognized that was precious to him and to me. He hadn't lived at home for five years, and I was surprised he'd kept so many little keepsakes around. I kept looking up and expecting him to walk through the door; I begged him to walk through the door. Maybe this was all a mistake—maybe it wasn't really Bryan who was killed! I can't even tell you how many times I prayed for that to be true.

Much of his clothing we packed separately and gave to Goodwill. Some of the larger items, like his furniture and television, we left for his roommates. In retrospect I wish I had brought all of his clothing and smaller items home. Later I realized just how precious every single item was. We piled the boxes into the back of

Bryan's little red Ford Ranger, and Dwaine and Jere set out on the long drive back to Idaho in Bryan's truck.

The coroner said they couldn't release Bryan to us until later in the week because it was a murder investigation. There was nothing left in Los Angeles for us to do, so Danetta and I flew home the next morning.

CHAPTER THREE
The Burial

Why is it that it's always good to be home again? Even under such tragic circumstances, and even knowing the awful days that were ahead of us, it was so good to be home. I walked into our home, Bryan's home, and there waiting for us were Steven, Jade and Whitney, Jade's husband, Kyle, their brand new, one-month-old baby, Tayler, and my friend Lynn. While we had been in Los Angeles, they and many other beloved friends and family had begun making the funeral and burial arrangements for us. Over the next few days the house was filled with people. Food and drink miraculously appeared, and I was never alone. I think they were afraid to leave me alone. As they should have been, I suppose. We occupied those early days with all the decisions that needed to be made. Where to hold the memorial service, what songs to play, what words to say, where Bryan's final resting place should be.

Because we had been in Los Angeles since the afternoon of the day that Bryan was killed, we were not aware that the local media had continued to report the events of our son's murder. Bryan's picture was on the morning and evening news, in the newspaper, on the internet. In Boise and in Los Angeles, the story ran solidly for weeks. And on and off again for the next twelve months until Bryan's killer was convicted and sentenced. The media interviewed my husband, my sister, my son-in-law, my sister-in-law. They wanted the details of the memorial service, in fact they actually came to the service and tried to interview more people there. They were not allowed inside. We'd had enough, and we wanted our privacy. There is something just wrong about turning on the TV and seeing your child's photo with the caption *"Slain Eagle High Student . . ."* No parent should have to experience that jolting pain, again and again.

Bryan's body finally arrived and was prepared for an open casket viewing for family and friends the night before the funeral. His father and I had agreed that we would each go sit with Bryan that morning; Jere would go first and call me when he was ready to leave, and then I would take my turn. I was looking forward to spending time with my son, to being alone with him. I planned to hold him, to kiss his cheek, and to tell him how much I loved him. I planned to sit with him all afternoon until they kicked me out.

Jere called much earlier than expected. He was upset. "Will you come down here right now?" he asked. With no hesitation, I said, "I'm on my way." Without even drying my hair (which quite honestly NEVER happens) I got in my car. My friend Jill happened to be pulling up to my house at that very moment, unplanned, and after quickly summarizing my state of mind, refused to let me drive. I gratefully got in her car and let her drive me to the funeral home.

I walked into the viewing room. I could see the casket in my peripheral vision, but I couldn't look at it yet. I just looked at my son's father. "What's wrong?" He had such a pained look in his eyes and gave me a big hug. I turned away and looked at the casket, took a long look at the lifeless body lying there. *No—no—this isn't right! This isn't Bryan!* Moaning, my legs collapsed, and I just kept screaming, "It isn't Bryan, it isn't Bryan, it doesn't look like Bryan!"

I was dimly aware that the funeral home folks had come in to see what was going on, then quietly closed the doors to muffle our cries. They told me later that they had never heard such primal pain in anyone's voice as they heard coming from me that day. Jere and I just collapsed into each other and held each other tightly, both of us sobbing. I continued screaming and moaning, "Bryan, Bryan, Bryan . . . "

The mortician had done his best, but too much time had gone by since Bryan's last breath. Because he had been in a fight and was murdered, his body was bruised and cut. In their efforts to make him look better, the end result was that my son was barely recognizable. After a long time, when I was able to stand on my own two feet again, I let Jere go and walked back over to my son.

I touched his hand. I looked at him for a long time, trying to see some resemblance to the vibrant young man we had raised. I recognized his bushy eyebrows and his hands. And of course, I recognized the suit we had provided for him. That was about it. I tried so hard to see the handsome, happy-go-lucky boy we knew, with the twinkling blue eyes and slightly crooked grin. Maybe a slight resemblance? I couldn't bear to look any longer—I kissed his hand and turned away.

"We can't let the others see him like this!" I exclaimed. "It will destroy them." I was particularly worried about the effect it would have on Bryan's step siblings, Steven, Jade, Chris, Brooke, and Whitney, all of whom were so very close to Bryan. (Chris and Brooke are Danetta's children—we have a very extended family between all of us.) So we instructed the funeral home to close the casket. At the viewing that night, many people were wondering why we made the change, but no one dared ask.

The memorial service the next day went as planned, except that we weren't prepared for the number of people who came to pay their respects to Bryan. The place was packed. There wasn't even standing room—friends and family filled all of the hallways and the kitchen and the offices and even spilled outside. So many people came to honor Bryan. It was beautiful and overwhelming, and he would have been so proud. I know I was.

I think we did a good job of expressing our love for Bryan

during the service and letting people know who he was and what he was about. His cousin Kevin put together a beautiful slide show of Bryan's life. The burial afterward was moving and tender. Bryan was bestowed with military honors because of his time at West Point, and we had bagpipes there to play "Amazing Grace," my favorite hymn. At the end, his family and closest friends each laid a long-stemmed yellow rose on his casket. Perhaps the most memorable and haunting scene from that day is the image I have of his eight friends from USC sitting on the bench directly behind the gravesite with the saddest and most forlorn looks on their faces. That picture will forever be etched in my memory.

Afterward we had a celebration of life event at our home that continued well into the next morning. Thankfully, Bryan's out-of-town friends kept us busy and occupied over the following couple of days. We had transformed the basement rec room, previously Bryan and Steven's domain, into a dorm room. We laid out piles of sleeping bags and blankets and pillows for the kids to sleep on. We stayed up late, laughed a lot, told endless stories, watched home movies, and we cried. We rented a trolley and went on a "field trip" of Bryan's life. We saw the house he was born in (where his father still lives), went to Boise State University and tossed a football on the famous blue turf that Bryan's beloved Boise State Broncos call home, ate ice cream, went to Bryan's high school and played more football there. We came home and had Bryan's favorite Mexican restaurant deliver food for everyone. We listened to his favorite band, Led Zeppelin, all day. Some of Bryan's closest high school friends were with us also, as well as family members. It was such an amazing time for all of us. As a group we were able to celebrate his life together, while revisiting many of our individual memories.

Inevitably though, the kids all went home, friends and family stopped coming by, and there were no more casseroles or flowers being delivered—there was just The Silence. And The Tears. So. Many. Tears. And The Pain. You know the kind of pain where your entire body hurts and your stomach feels like you've been run over by a train? The kind of pain where you can't breathe? I was so heartbroken for Bryan. So sad that he wouldn't be able to accomplish his dreams. He would never see graduation from film school, he would never marry, he would never have children, he would never even have a career. Bryan was a very driven and accomplished young man. From the day he was born he was off and running, always seeking greater learning and higher truths for himself. *This is so unfair! Why has this happened to us?* I cried to myself. *I believe in God; I try to be a good person. Why us? Why Bryan? Why my child?* I was a successful real estate broker by trade. But I had no interest in returning to work. I handed over all of my clients and pending contracts to a colleague, and I stayed home.

I stayed home with my pain and my memories. I started drinking wine in the afternoon and became obsessed with burning questions. *Did he have any pain, how could I not have known, is he in Heaven, why did this have to happen, why Bryan; he didn't deserve to die; how will I go on?* And more questions. *Is this even real? Am I dreaming? How will I survive this? What do I do now, if not be Bryan's mom?* I had no answers, so I just cried and shut myself off to the world. I immersed myself in my memories. That's all I had left, right? And I drank more wine.

I organized all of the photographs I had of Bryan on my computer and scanned earlier pictures so that I would have them in digital format. Then I created a variety of digital memory books—one for Bryan's father and paternal grandparents, another for his step siblings, one for my own father and siblings, and yet another one for his friends at USC. I found someone to convert all of our old video camera tapes to DVDs so that I could watch them more easily, and so that they would be preserved forever. I thought a lot about my mother and my grandparents, who had also passed. I bought photo collage frames in bulk. I would walk by Bryan's bedroom in the basement where we had stored all of his belongings, but I couldn't bear to go inside. I found everything he ever wrote, his poems and papers and such all the way back to preschool and organized them also. I pulled together all of the cards he had given me over the years, and I read and re-read them again and again. I played his favorite music all day; I wore his clothes and his necklace; I talked to him; I sat on my front porch wrapped in blankets, and I drank wine and listened to the songs from the funeral over and over again. I cried myself to sleep and I woke up crying every day. I begged God to give me answers to my questions.

I was afraid, you see. Afraid of a life without my son, and afraid of whether or not his life continued on beyond this life, the one we knew.

I remember one day in particular, sitting on the floor in my living room, an almost empty bottle of wine beside me. It was cold outside, so I had moved myself, my wine, and my music indoors. John Lennon's "Beautiful Boy" blared in the room around me, and for the first time I screamed at God. I sobbed, I pounded the floor, I was writhing in pain. And then I begged Him, *Please bring him back. Please! Take me, take me instead. I will do anything, God—anything at all! Please bring him back to me.* I remember even thinking about making a deal with the Devil himself, but I did stop short of that. I wasn't completely lost, I guess. But I sat there and cried and screamed and tried to negotiate with God to bring back my dead son.

Death seemed so final to me then. I really couldn't comprehend it. *What do you mean I'll never see or talk to my son again? WHAT?* I couldn't imagine one more day without him, much less another week or month or year. I didn't understand—on one hand I always knew that there was such a thing as life after death, but I didn't really believe it. Did I?

I could never have predicted what would happen next.

CHAPTER FOUR

Mom!

*J*ust a few weeks after Bryan passed, I was lying on my bed at home one evening waiting for Dwaine to finish in the bathroom. I was in that light, hypnotic, alpha state of not quite asleep and not quite awake, when I heard "MOMMMMMM!" I heard Bryan's voice call out for me as clearly as if he were standing right next to me. The word was very drawn out and, although it sounded a little like his younger boy voice, I knew it was Bryan. I heard him out loud—with my ears—not inside of my head. My immediate thought was worry—worry that he sounded scared or frightened—natural reactions for a mother who didn't know where her son had gone and whether or not he was in pain. I later understood that he was practically screaming at me in order to break through my heavy grief so that I could hear him. I can only imagine how many times he had tried before.

"BRYAN!" I sat up and listened for more. Nothing. But I had all I needed. In that moment, that nanosecond—when my self-perceived barriers that had separated us blessedly melted away—I heard my son. I heard my son! In an instant, I was on a mission to find him. To find my son who had been murdered at the age of twenty-three. My son and only living birth child. My Bryan.

Can you imagine the joy I felt at hearing my son's voice again? The pain and heartache of living with the death of a child is unsurpassed, in my opinion. It simply is not in the correct order of things that our children die before us. It is wrong. It is unbearable. It tears us completely apart. It hurts SO bad, day after day after day. There is no way to make sense of the how and the why of it.

So, while I could fill pages and pages right now, describing in further detail my pain to you, and telling you all about my deep sadness, I want to tell you about the healing. My healing, and my family's healing. It all began with that one word. When my son called out to me from somewhere that I couldn't see—MOM!

For I knew at that moment in time that I could still have a relationship with my son. I also intuitively knew it would be the only way I would survive this tragedy. And so, I set out to find him. I promised him that I would not stop looking.

And find him I did.

CHAPTER FIVE
Becoming a Seeker

The questions that had been burning inside of me started to get louder and become even more persistent. Now that I knew he was SOMEWHERE, I had to know more. *Where is he? Does this mean there IS life after death, and what does that really mean, anyway? Is he here with me now? Can he hear me?* I was particularly worried about whether or not Bryan was in heaven, in part because of his voice that I heard call out to me *(How could I have heard his voice? Does that mean he isn't in heaven at all, but rather is "stuck" somewhere, like in the movie Ghost?)* and partly because he never professed a relationship with God. His friend Kamal later told me that he believed Bryan "found God" during their trip to the Himalayan Mountains in Pakistan the summer before he died. Bryan shared with Kamal that he couldn't deny the presence of a divine being after seeing the glory and beauty of the Himalayan Mountains. I can't tell you how much relief and joy I felt when I heard that, and I am eternally grateful to Kamal for sharing it with me.

My questions were relentless, and I needed answers. I went to the bookstore and bought a variety of books. I didn't know what I was looking for specifically, my only requirement was that the books be about the subject of life after death. I had heard my son out loud with my ears—he must still exist! The first book I read was George Anderson's *Lessons from the Light*. George Anderson is a world-renowned psychic medium, and in the book he recounts astonishing, beautiful and hopeful spirit communications from lost loved ones.

Shortly after Thanksgiving, a few weeks after devouring *Lessons from the Light*, I thought to myself, *I need to find a medium*. I had not had this thought one time prior to that moment, even while reading the book, yet the urgency of that thought is still with me today. My mind flashed on a local psychic I had heard on the radio a number of years back, and I remembered at the time thinking he was either the real deal or a very good con artist!

No more than two days later, Dwaine and I were at the grocery store, in the produce section. I looked up and saw the parents of one of Bryan's friends from high school. We knew the family fairly well because their son and our daughter Jade had dated for a couple of years. I remember saying to myself, *I should go say hi*, but I didn't want to—I didn't want to see the pity on their faces. It was enough that I had left the house—I had been having panic attacks every time I ventured too far from my safe haven. I kept hearing, *Go talk to them* in my head, and yet I resisted. Finally, the voice in my head was so loud that I said "Okay!" out loud. (I can only imagine what anyone standing near me was thinking about this crazy lady who was talking to no one.) I walked up, said hello, and reminded them who I was. The woman replied, "Paige, of course I remember you. How is Bryan?" OH MY GOD. Oh my God! She didn't know. They didn't know! I began to cry and then told them what had happened. They were shocked. How had they missed hearing about it? I don't know, but their son was in college in another state, so he had not known either. She proceeded to tell me that she had been doing a lot of spiritual development work and to let her know if she could help me at all. Jokingly, I asked if she knew of a good psychic. She replied, "As a matter of fact I do." Then she told me about a man named David Akins who lives in an adjacent community to ours, who as it turns out is the same man I had heard on the radio years before. No coincidences, right?

She continued to tell me that she was hosting a group message circle at her home in a few weeks, that this gentleman would be there providing messages from Spirit, and said she had two spots open if I wanted them. I felt like I was riding one of those moving tracks like you see at an airport—things were definitely out of my control. I was clearly not in charge of the events that were unfolding, but I knew enough to go with the flow and let things roll. I have to say that it actually felt damn good to resign myself to the belief that something or someone bigger than me was taking over—what a relief that was. I was curious, excited, and terrified.

And of course, I said yes.

That message circle opened my eyes to a whole new world. A world where our souls live on after death. A world where our loved ones are always right beside us, guiding us and helping us in our times of need. A world where some psychic mediums are the real deal, and communication with "the other side" IS possible.

I asked Lynn to go with me. We walked into this couple's home, not knowing any of the other guests. We grazed lightly on refreshments and made small talk but let me tell you—I was wound up tighter than an eight-day clock. When the medium arrived, he greeted everyone but made no small talk. He was not given any advance information about the guests in attendance, not even first names. The guests were only known to the host of the message circle. We sat ourselves randomly in a semicircle in her living room, with David and his assistant at the front.

David opened his message circle with psychic predictions and spiritual insights for the group as a whole, generally speaking about current affairs. After that he randomly selected individuals for their readings; he didn't go in a line, so it was nerve-racking wondering when my turn would be. The other participants listened to each person's reading, which averaged ten to fifteen minutes in length. After four or five others, he finally turned to me. My heart was beating so loudly I was sure everyone in the room could hear it. David began by saying that an older, tall and thin gentleman was stepping forward and then described my much-beloved Paw-Paw, my paternal grandfather. I started to get excited, then David said,

"He has a young man with him; he is bringing forward your son."

As I received the words that my son spoke through David that night, I was mesmerized. My heart continued to pound, and I hung onto every word he said. My grief was still raw—my heart still in pieces. The entire room was so still you could hear a pin drop—I think everyone in the room could feel my pain, as well as the love coming from my son. David told the events of Bryan's passing, even relaying the names of the two boys who were with him on the street that night. Those boys' names were never released in the media, not one time to my knowledge. He also described my son's physical appearance. Bryan apologized to me for dying but said that he knew he wouldn't live to be old. He said my mother, who passed in 2002, had been helping him a lot. David said that I had felt odd or out of sorts the day or the day before Bryan was killed. (Remember in my phone conversation with Bryan the night before he died when I had told him I didn't feel well?) The information was so accurate that I had no choice but to believe it was real.

Please remember that David is not provided with the names of anyone in attendance at his message circles prior to the readings. I know this to be true because I have since held my own message circles with him, and never did I provide him with the names of those who would be attending. It is not possible that he could have researched me or Bryan prior to that reading.

So—there it was. How could I deny the evidence that was presented to me in that living room that night? David gave me what I so desperately needed. Proof that my son did still exist! He was still near me and he was real, and I could communicate with him. He was not gone! I couldn't see him or touch him, but just the thought of him still being accessible to me was all I needed at that moment. A light was shown to me that night, a pathway toward healing, a bread crumb on the trail of this horrible journey called grief, and I knew which way to turn. I never looked back after that night.

When you're willing to tread beyond the limits of logic, you swim in the presence of your loved one. Dismiss the limits of logic, dismiss what you think you always knew—look away from what the thinking mind is projecting and see what the universe is bringing forth. Don't look back; go forward with trust and in faith.

CHAPTER SIX

Bryan, Is That You?

With the door to the wonders of the afterlife cracked open, our family started experiencing signs of Bryan's presence all around us—signs, signs, so many signs! The more we paid attention, the more signs we would receive. I can only imagine how thrilled he was to finally be getting through to us.

Crazy things started happening. My iPod would begin playing by itself, Bryan's favorite songs would be on the radio when I started the car engine. I had dreams in which I would have sworn he was with me in real time. Pictures of him would flash on my cell phone home screen then disappear again. I would see shadow movements in the corner of rooms. Our TV would turn off and on again. Our list of miracles is long. Particularly in the first couple of years, Bryan worked so hard to let us know he was still with us.

Thankfully, someone suggested I keep a journal of what I came to call my "Bryan Miracles," which I did for the first year and a half after his death. Here are some of our favorites:

December 18, 2008: We went to my stepdaughter's house for an early Christmas celebration. (My husband and I had decided to escape to the beach for the holidays because we just couldn't face them without Bryan.) Since Jade had birthed our first grandchild in August of that year, Bryan was able to meet little Tayler over the summer while he was home visiting. I've always been grateful for that visit. It means so much to me that at least one of our grandkids knew Bryan. Tayler remains connected to Bryan to this very day, and in fact her two sisters talk about playing with Bryan "while they were in heaven together." Their sweet little faces light up with joy when they see how happy that makes me!

That evening we had all been sitting in the living room, playing with the baby and talking about whether or not Bryan was in the room celebrating with us. All of a sudden, a wooden decoration—a plaque that read "It's not about the presents, it's about HIS presence"— fell off the wall from where it was hanging above the sliding glass doors. We laughed, acknowledged Bryan, and toasted him. The following month, during a group message circle at my home, I asked David Akins if Bryan had been with us that December night. Bryan told David that there was a candle burning (there was) and said "toasting." Yes, he was with us all right!

February 20, 2009: When my husband got home after work, I told him I had just had an amazing Bryan experience, but he didn't ask me about it or express much interest. Later in the evening I asked him why he didn't ask about it, was he tired of hearing about all this spiritual stuff? Right then I looked at the TV—it was frozen on the screen—as if a DVR recording was on but had been paused. I looked at the remote in my hand and wondered if I had paused it, so I pressed the play and fast forward buttons numerous times, but the screen remained frozen. We commented, "Wow—look at that! The TV won't start playing—maybe it's Bryan doing this" and then Dwaine said, "Okay, I want to hear your Bryan story, tell me." And at that instant the TV came back on! I believe Bryan was letting us know he was with us, and also that he wanted Dwaine to stay on this journey with me.

May 10, 2009: The first year without your loved one is full of so many painful firsts. The first birthday without him, the first Christmas without him, the first anniversary of his death, etc. This was my first Mother's Day without Bryan. I have always loved Mother's Day. Maybe in part because Bryan was my only living child, I really loved to celebrate being his mom. Most years, when Bryan still lived at home, he would spend the day working on my latest landscape project with me. On this Mother's Day in 2009 I woke up crying uncontrollably, so deep was my sadness. I decided to meditate (a new practice of mine). I set the TV to mute, and quickly felt myself relax into the stillness and the quiet. I prayed that God and my angels would help my spirit guides and loved ones (specifically Bryan) to come through with whatever message

I needed to receive that day. Eventually I started to feel tingly all over and I felt pressure at the back of my head. My feet felt heavy as I focused on them being planted on the ground. I didn't see or hear anything for a long time, then I started to notice a white light growing and growing, then break into small hearts that were swirling and drifting around. I kept thinking *Read God's word*, but I thought that was crazy at that moment, and I didn't want to do it. I finished the meditation disappointed, thinking I had received nothing.

Next I went into the garage to gather up some items that I needed, and suddenly had the thought that I should at least get my Bible and open it and see what page I landed on. I went back inside and on the TV were the words, "Hurry. Offer Ends Soon." Hilarious, right? *All right, I'll do it.* I got my Bible from the bedroom and held it against my chest. I noticed there was a card in it, so I removed the card so as not to influence where I opened the pages to read my message from God. I was so excited and was trying to intuit exactly where I should part the pages. When I did finally open the Bible, all I saw were some passages, meaningless to me at that moment. No message there that I could see, so I tried again, but again nothing was relevant. No earth shattering, divine messages. In defeat, I closed the Bible and picked up the card that I had removed and set aside: it was a handmade Mother's Day card from Bryan from 1995. He had drawn small hearts all over it, exactly like the ones in my meditation. *Thank you, thank you, thank you.* This was the message I'd so desperately needed that day—I'd needed to be assured that Bryan is still with me, that I am still his mother and I can still have a loving relationship with him.

July 12, 2009: I had been thinking about Bryan all morning and had been crying. Eventually I got myself together, got ready for work, and got in my car. Just as I was putting the key in the ignition, I felt his presence. *Bryan, you're here! You're here!* His presence was so strong and powerful. I talked to him for a minute then had a strong urge to turn on the radio. Journey's hit song "Don't Stop Believing" was playing, followed by Captain & Tennille's "Love Will Keep Us Together." You can't make this stuff up, friends!

November 25, 2010: This is not so much a sign from Bryan, rather proof that he was still hanging around with us. My husband and I were visiting Jade and her family in Salt Lake City for Thanksgiving. They had moved to Salt Lake City earlier in the year, and we missed them desperately. Tayler was two years old now and had never built a snowman. Luckily there was lots of snow that year, so we bundled up and went outside and had such fun. After building the snowman we came in the house to warm up and have hot chocolate. We were all seated around the kitchen table drinking our hot chocolate when suddenly our granddaughter pointed and said "Hey! Everyone is drinking hot chocolate except that guy over there!" "Over there" was the empty chair at the table. "That guy," of course, was Bryan.

We all had chills running up and down our spines as we felt his presence with us at the table. Just knowing that this sweet two-year-old child could SEE him blew us away. How could we ever deny or question the truth of an afterlife after this?

In **2014** I opened Crystal Soul Healing Center in Boise. While the Center itself was rather short-lived, it provided so much healing for me and for others while it was open. One October morning I asked Bryan for a sign that he was by my side, supporting me with the Healing Center. Instantly I felt him next to me and I knew that yes, of course, he is supporting me and cheering me on. But I still said (out loud), "Okay, I know, but still can you send me a sign, please?"

A couple of days later, after a long day of getting the Center ready for the grand opening, I finally got home and checked my front porch to see if a delivery I'd been waiting for had come. I saw a box next to the door. I picked it up, thinking the box was too small to hold the items I had ordered. When I looked at the label, I saw the box was addressed to Brian Frost (different spelling but the name is the same!) The package should have gone to a Brian Frost who lived in a different community. Strange? I think not— remember, no coincidences! Spirit will use anything or anyone available to deliver our messages.

February 2017: I'd been trying to get Phantom of the Opera tickets for my granddaughter and me for at least forty minutes. The website crashed and the box office phone kept sending me to a recording. I took a deep breath, said a quick prayer and asked nicely for a real person to answer the phone. I called again and a nice young man named BRYAN answered the phone and got my tickets for me. Floor, front row, middle seats. Boom! This actually happens quite frequently—when working with a stranger over the phone who is working on some kind of problem for me, chances are pretty good that his name will be Bryan!

e open. Each one of you can ask for signs from your loved ones in Spirit. They are waiting with great anticipation for you to simply ask! You just need to open your heart and your mind and BELIEVE—have faith that all things are possible! And then watch— be alert—pay attention to what is happening around you. Live in the moment because that's where Spirit resides within you. If you allow your thoughts to constantly live in the past or project into the future, you will miss the miracles that are here for you NOW.

CHAPTER SEVEN

Asking for Signs

*C*learly, Bryan had begun sending signs on his own. After all, he knew what I needed and what was possible from the very first. But my first REQUEST for Bryan to send me a sign came about on a beautiful early August morning in 2009.

I was working in my garden, pulling weeds and pruning flowers. I felt a strong presence surrounding me, accompanied by that very strange and unsettling feeling of being watched. This lasted for about twenty minutes. I kept looking around, expecting to see my husband or neighbor, but of course no one was there. I looked around again and called out "All right, who is here? Mom? Bryan?" No response. "Mom, if this is you, please send me a yellow butterfly!" Nothing. "Okay, Bryan if this is you, please send me a . . . uh . . . a ladybug!" Nothing. I chuckled to myself and wondered where THAT came from. I had no particular affinity for ladybugs and I certainly didn't really believe that one would suddenly appear. Then my negativity was replaced with "Trust that you have asked for this miracle and it will appear. When it does you will be SO happy."

Well, ok, I thought with relief, and went about my day.

That evening our kids and grandbaby came over to celebrate my fiftieth birthday. By then I had completely forgotten about my earlier experience in the garden, and I was busy preparing dinner and visiting with the kids. I was walking by the bay window in the dining room and suddenly I started screaming and jumping up and down and yelling Bryan's name—there on the windowsill was a ladybug! The kids and my husband didn't know what was happening because first of all, I hadn't told them about my experience in the garden, and second, they didn't see the ladybug right away. They thought I had completely lost my mind—maybe they thought I was having another panic attack. I just kept screaming and thanking Bryan over and over again.

I had never seen a ladybug in my house before this, and we had been living there for eleven years. Since that day, we have received many, many ladybugs. Always at a special family gathering one of us will find a ladybug gently resting on us or sitting at our table. At Steven's rehearsal dinner, at his wedding, on our granddaughter's birthday, while sitting at the cemetery, on a California beach in March, in Hawaii while sharing emotions about Bryan with my husband, on the very chilly top deck of a cruise ship in Glacier Bay,

Alaska—ladybugs and more ladybugs. Is every ladybug we see from Bryan? No, of course not. But most of them are. And we know they are because we always get that chill up and down our spine when it is really from him. I call it a "spiritual tingle." Sometimes he sends them "just because," like receiving flowers from your special love when it's not Valentine's Day or your birthday. Usually the ladybug will sit with us for a little while and then fly away, never to be seen again. I still get excited every time. It has become Bryan's fun, special way to let us know he is still with us.

I have to share with you one more ladybug story. On October 1, 2012, my dad died. I loved my dad so much. I have always been a daddy's girl, my entire life. He had started to show signs of dementia settling in over the year or so prior to his death, and my siblings and I were helping him out by paying his bills for him, doing his grocery shopping, managing his medications, etc. But in the summer of 2012 my dad started to decline very rapidly; we were completely unprepared and totally overwhelmed.

On September 24, 2012 Dad had been admitted into the hospital again. It was his second or third hospital visit that summer. On that morning my phone had decided it wouldn't hold a charge anymore, so off I went to Verizon for a new phone. This is right when the newest iPhone was just coming out. The sales associates practically laughed at me for thinking I could walk away with a new iPhone that very day; they said it was a three-week wait. "But I have to have a phone today," I said. The employee at the counter expressed some sympathy for my situation and said, "Well, maybe we have one in the back—oops no we don't. But Fed Ex just got here and there is supposed to be a 64-gig, white phone in the box that I don't think is spoken for."

YAY! I get excited—this is the exact phone I want to buy. But no—they call the manager and he says it is for someone else. Deflated, we resume our back-up planning, which is becoming quite complicated. So then, in walks the manager ON HIS DAY OFF, and next thing I know, hooray, the new, white iPhone is NOT for anyone else, and it's mine. I am so happy of course, but it gets better. Then I say, "I need a cover." The manager picks up a box and says, "Well, how about this ladybug cover?" Seriously? It was the coolest! Red with ladybug markings all over it.

I told him all about Bryan and that he sends me ladybugs and I KNOW Bryan has made sure that I get that phone that day, so I wouldn't miss any important calls about my dad. I think even those employees might have become believers in the afterlife that day. All I know is three hours later, I walked out with my ladybug iPhone in my hand, off to see my dad with a big grin on my face and so much love and gratitude for my Bryan.

When you open yourself up to the possibility
of your loved ones still being alive and still being
accessible to you, the most amazing things begin to
happen. Naysayers might call them coincidences;
I choose to call them miracles, and I hope you will
too. Your loved ones want to bridge the dimensional
barriers to commune with you and are quite
creative in their efforts to do so. Can you feel it?
Do you want it? Say yes. Just say yes and invite
them in!

Chapter Eight
Finding Spirituality

Following that first group message circle with the parents of Bryan's friend, I became a seeker of all things related to the afterlife. Really, it started with his calling out to me—MOM! The drive to understand what I couldn't see or touch became everything to me. I was obsessed with needing to find my son. Now that I knew it was possible, I was off and running. Bryan's frequent signs fueled my own insatiable need to learn more.

Many of the books I'd been reading about the afterlife talked about "spirituality" and "being spiritual." These words were becoming a big part of my awareness, but the truth is that I didn't really understand what they meant. My four siblings and I were raised Presbyterian, although we were not regular church goers at all. More like Sunday School classes when we were little, and our parents would gather us all up for Easter services, my four siblings and I proudly displayed in our new dresses and outfits, my sisters and I complete with little white gloves and purses. So, as an adult I didn't really know what my beliefs were. I know I believed in the concept of a "God." I thought Heaven and Hell were places "up there" or "down there," and which one we ultimately went to was determined by how well we behaved in this life. Bryan and I had visited many churches together over the years but none of them were right for us. None of them made us feel like *yes this is our truth, we are home."* I remember in his sophomore year of high school we went to Catholic mass and it was all I could do to remain seated for the entire service. I left feeling less-than, and not worthy of God. That is not to judge all the good Catholics out there— to each his own. It just wasn't for me. Neither was Presbyterian, or Lutheran, or Baptist, or Quaker, or bible study classes—all different types of religious attire that I tried on. None of them fit. I also didn't have firm beliefs about the afterlife before Bryan died, other than a very general belief in "life after death"—a belief with no substance or experience behind it.

So, this new spiritual awareness and unfolding of proof that the afterlife exists was intriguing and curious to me. From the moment I heard my son call out to me, my healing journey became one of *being willing to be open and to explore—even those things that I didn't understand.* I knew I had God by my side. I have never wavered in my belief that God exists. Not when my beloved grandparents each died, not when my baby girl Jamie died in my womb after 6 months of pregnancy, and not when I lost two other babies in early pregnancy. Not when my mom died at the age of sixty-six, not when my friend died of a brain aneurysm in his thirties, and not when my dad died in 2012. In fact, I had known God to work in my life in many ways. He had saved my life, and Bryan's, on multiple occasions.

The most compelling example of this happened in the spring of 1992. Friends of mine were rafting the mighty Lochsa River in north central Idaho. The Lochsa, which means Rough Water in the native Nez Perce language, is ferocious and explosive white water, for hard-core rafters only. My friends were experienced rafters, well equipped to handle this raging river that was running high and strong with run-off from the previous winter's snow. I was not an experienced rafter, however, so my friend asked if I would station myself below one of the rapids and photograph the raft coming through the rapid. I thought that sounded like a fun and safe adventure, so I said yes and took Bryan with me. Bryan was seven years old then. We had the best time on the drive from Boise, singing out loud to The Beatles all the way. We met my friends at their put-in spot, then my friend Ron drove us to the place downriver where I was to take the photographs. He gave me a quick lesson on how to use his camera, a very expensive and professional looking camera with a zoom attachment on it. I placed the camera around my neck, put a life jacket on Bryan, and headed to our waiting spot. We situated ourselves on some large boulders that lined the banks of the river—it was almost like a wall of boulders. We were fairly high up above the river to my recollection—I remember looking DOWN onto the river. We were perched on our boulder, talking, waiting for sounds from the rafters to signal they were getting close. I was fiddling around with the camera, and I didn't notice that Bryan had moved from his spot until, suddenly, I heard him cry out. I jumped up, saw instantly that he had fallen into the river, and I jumped. I didn't think, I didn't have a plan, I just jumped. Camera, sunglasses, and all. Thank God I landed close to Bryan and was able to grab onto his life jacket. We were only about six feet from the rock wall where we'd been seated, and I started to swim. I am a good swimmer. I lived in Las Vegas, Nevada for eight years as a teenager and I swam almost every day. But this river was strong, and the water was deep and freezing cold. And I only had one arm to swim with. Still, I did my best, trying to get us to shore but we were going nowhere. I realized then that we were stuck in an eddy, which is a circular movement of water, counter to a main current, that causes a small whirlpool. My next thoughts were *I'm freezing, I don't have a life jacket on, and I don't think I can fight this water for much longer. Please God, help us.*

I can't explain what happened next. I don't even know. One minute we were in the water, me desperately holding on to Bryan with one hand and trying to swim with the other. The next moment we were back on the rocks—wet, shaken, and almost in a hypothermic state, *but alive and clinging to one other*. I prayed right then and there, thanking God for saving us. There was no explanation for this miracle, other than to accept that the hand of God, or one of His angels, reached into that river and plucked us out of that deadly water, placing us safely back on the rocks. The camera and sunglasses were lost, but we were alive. We were alive!

Truly a miraculous event, one that I can recall today as clearly as if it had just happened yesterday.

So yes, I have known God in my life. And when Bryan died, my belief that God exists still did not waver. Although, believe me, I questioned why we were saved so many years ago, just to have Bryan die sixteen years later. I can only believe that he wasn't done yet, he and I both had things yet to accomplish; it wasn't our time then to die.

But believing in God was one thing; having experienced God's work in my life was wonderful. *Yet consciously living a spiritual life with God at the helm*—well this was something new for me to explore.

Boy, did I explore! And those explorations (the seeking) became my pathway to healing from the death of my child. As I studied, learned to discern what my truths were, and continued to put one foot forward (even though sometimes I would fall two steps back), I began to feel Bryan around me in ways that I hadn't before. I started to become aware of God and the Universe in ways that I had never known before.

It didn't happen right away, but I did develop my own unique understanding of spirituality. It unfolded slowly, beautifully, in divine beauty and with divine timing. Imagine a lotus flower, each petal shining brightly and ever so slowly, opening—reaching up to touch the golden warmth of the sun's rays. This was me, reaching up to feel God's love and the love from my son. I'm sure there were times when I got the two of them confused, so desperate was I to make that other-worldly connection. What I discovered, though, was an unconditionally loving God who embraced me, who forgave me my mishaps, and who nurtured my spiritual awakening. Who would never give me more than I could bear. Who brought me teachers when I was ready for new awareness. Who has gifted me with the most beautiful communications from and with my son. Who has shown me such insight into who I really am, and a glimpse into why I have had the many hardships I've had in my life.

As I became more and more comfortable with these new beliefs, I began to be aware of my spiritual team guiding me, helping me, coaxing me along toward new ideas and higher truths. I came to identify all of these beings collectively as Spirit. To me, Spirit is All That Is. Spirit is God, Spirit is All of the Angels and Archangels. Spirit is Bryan, Spirit is my mom and my dad and my grandparents. Spirit is your loved ones as well. Spirit is Love. I came to understand that with God, all things are possible. *Bryan's death had become the catalyst for my spiritual awakening.* Now, after death, he continues to walk by my side.

The beauty of awakening your soul is a conscious choice for you to make. Spirit might offer the opportunity for awakening, but it is up to you to say yes and to allow it. The joy of discovering God and your loved ones in Spirit is but a breath away—a prayer to ask them to guide you and to help ease your pain. Your version of God might look different from others'; your version of God might not even carry the same name. What is important is to reach out for what you believe in—ask for divine guidance and assistance and it shall be given to you.

CHAPTER NINE

Opening Your Intuition

*A*rmed with my newly discovered glimpses into spirituality and the afterlife, and with my God and my Bryan at my side, I launched into the next phase of my journey.

I began by signing up for psychic development classes, taught by the same man who had given me the first message circle reading. I felt like I was supposed to be there, and I knew Bryan was guiding me. I was so excited! I walked into the classroom, taking a seat in the front row. I have always been one of those kids—the one who sits in the front row and is never afraid to raise her hand to ask a question of the teacher.

There were fifteen or twenty people seated in the room, with the teacher and his assistant sitting at the front. David Akins is an extraordinary man. Not only is he a well-renowned psychic medium, but he is an ordained minister who founded a local church in his community. He is a large man with a beard and hair that falls below his shoulders. He has a booming voice, an entertaining twinkle in his eyes, and an infectious laugh. Not your typical church pastor by any means! David is passionate about the work he does, and he is absolutely unapologetic to critics and non-believers about his psychic abilities. So, although I sat in the front row this first night of his class, I was a little scared and intimidated by this giant of a man. Within moments, however, I recognized David's love for God, prayer, and faith, and I felt how committed he was to helping each of us understand that *we are spiritual souls here on this earth having a human experience*—not the other way around. This, in itself, was new information for me, a wholly new and beautiful concept for me to explore and understand. Let me say it again. We are spiritual souls here on this earth having a human experience.

The second night of the class we practiced psychometry—the ability to discover facts about an event or person by touching inanimate objects associated with them. We were to write down everything we were intuitively receiving about that person while holding their possession. I was amazed to discover that much of what we received for each other was accurate. I had brought a necklace of Bryan's that he wore almost daily, it was a necklace that I bought for him when I traveled to Greece in 2006. The woman who "read" Bryan's necklace that night got so many things right. While meditating on the necklace she intuitively (mentally) received symbols which she in turn interpreted for me. She saw that

I was experiencing a rising of spiritual consciousness, she saw that I had a pain in my shoulder, she saw that I had financial stability in my life, and more. Most telling was when she said that her right hip was hurting. David was able to guide her through the meaning behind that pain, eventually getting us all to understand that the pain in her hip was a symbol for child loss, more specifically my child loss.

My reading was for another woman in the room who had brought a ring with her. From that item I was able to intuit information about a young child who had died, who turned out to be one of her daughter's best friends from childhood. I remember during the reading that I saw a little girl swinging on a backyard swing, and I was overcome with sadness and emotional pain.

So, if a complete stranger who wasn't a practiced psychic would know things about me simply by holding my son's necklace, and if I could know things about another woman's loved one simply by holding her ring, this could only mean that, indeed, we are all a little bit intuitive. It could only mean that every single one of us has some kind of psychic gift. A gift that, when in alignment with God, can provide healing for others. What? Now that was a game changer!

As the class was introductory and fairly basic, many of us chose to continue on with other workshops that David offered, such as Psychic Development II, an Angels & Guides workshop, and an Oracles workshop. The more I learned, the more determined I was to figure out how to communicate with Bryan directly. I was still in the first year of Bryan's death, and I couldn't get enough of these new spiritual teachings. Still being driven by the desire to continue having a relationship with my son, I forged ahead.

A group of seven of us who had attended the first development workshop together started what is commonly known as a psychic development circle. A psychic development circle contains a group of people who are all interested in improving their natural psychic abilities such as clairvoyance, psychometry, telepathy, mediumship, telekinesis, energy healing, and more. We met weekly in the evenings and almost never skipped a week, alternating the meeting location between several of our homes. We began by practicing more psychometry readings for each other and then advanced to intuitive readings using no "props." After about a year, we felt ready to invite guests into our circle and provide intuitive readings for them. We would start with a meditation; then we would each take a few moments and write down everything that came to us (mentally, physically or emotionally). Then we would take turns giving our readings to the guest. It was a fascinating time for me, for all of us, and to share my spiritual development with a group of like-minded friends felt special and magical to me. I loved every minute of our time together.

Our group naturally parted ways after about eighteen months of these weekly meetings. I am so grateful for the unconditional love and support that we gave each other. There was no judgment between us, we were all spiritual beings seeking a deeper understanding of who we are. We each had unique gifts that were beginning to unfold. The more we opened ourselves up to these gifts through practice and meditation, the more we trusted the information that came through, the more accurate the information was, and the more that was revealed.

Every one of us is intuitive. You each possess a unique gift that you brought with you to this life. Some of you might be more attuned to SEEING Spirit (clairvoyance), versus HEARING Spirit (clairaudience). Or you might be especially adept at FEELING Spirit (clairsentience), versus simply a KNOWING that something is true (claircognizance). In fact, most people possess one or more of these intuitive gifts. There are many ways that you can choose to strengthen your gifts, should you desire to do so.

We are spiritual souls here on this earth having a human experience. If we can remember that throughout our interactions with others and within ourselves, then life just doesn't seem so hard. Emotions like judgment and hate and condemnation simply melt away. Honor each person's unique journey in this life, including your own. Look at yourself and others as the beautiful soul being that you are. Embrace your spiritual gifts and trust the messages you will receive.

CHAPTER TEN
Pain and Suffering

There is a darker side to grief that many people don't want to talk about. The pain and suffering, the anger, the guilt, the blame—it must be felt and released, often many times over. We cannot bury these feelings and expect to heal. Sometimes people let their pain and suffering overcome them, and some of those people choose suicide as a way out of their pain. I am not judging that choice, but I want to share my experience regarding this topic with you.

One day in early summer of 2009 I was out driving my son's little red Ford Ranger truck. It had been about nine months since Bryan had died and up until then I hadn't been able to part with it. However, I had decided to sell the truck to my nephew, Bryan's younger cousin Kevin. But first I wanted one more joy ride, one more cruise with Bryan in his little red truck that he loved so much. We had driven all the way from Boise to Los Angeles in that truck together when he was starting his first semester of school at USC. We played classic rock on the radio and talked and laughed. We would rev the engine and get a running start on the big hill at Donner Pass because the truck didn't have enough power to get to the top otherwise. We made a game of it and had so much fun!

But on this day, I drove to a reservoir about twenty miles from my home, over a small mountain and through an adjacent farming community. We had taken the kids water skiing and boating at this reservoir many times over the years. So many picnics and so many hours watching them jump off the bridge into the cool waters below. As I drove, all of those sweet memories filled my mind. Led Zeppelin, our favorite band, was blaring on the radio. All of a sudden I wanted to be with Bryan so bad! As if in slow motion, I swerved the car sharply to the right, heading straight for the water. I remember thinking loudly (if a thought could be loud, this was it) *NO this is not what you want. This is NOT the way.* I corrected the truck, slowing down on the side of the road, just feet away from an embankment rising several feet above the reservoir. I felt defeated, and I shed many more tears that day. How would I ever heal? Would it ever get better? Would I ever get better? Did I want to die? Did I want to live?

Would I have died, had I driven into the water that day? Maybe, maybe not. Intuitively, though, I understood that I had needed to test myself in such a frightening way. I needed to put thoughts of suicide to rest because I kept thinking about whether or not it was an option for me.

I believe all parents who have experienced the death of a child probably become curious about suicide at one point or another. But that was not to be my path. Nor was drowning myself in a bottle. I'd tried that too. Having a family history of alcoholism, I was very conscious of how much I had begun drinking and decided early on in my journey to stop that abusive behavior. Besides, a drunken person can't connect with Spirit reliably; the alcohol numbs the senses too much.

In his book *A New Earth: Awakening to Your Life's Purpose*, Eckhart Tolle writes, "The fire of suffering becomes the light of consciousness. The ego says I shouldn't have to suffer and that thought makes you suffer so much more. It is a distortion of the truth, which is always paradoxical. The truth is that you need to say yes to suffering before you can transcend it."

Take the time to do the hard work. Grieve the loss of your loved one's physical presence. Grieve the loss of all your hopes and dreams that involved them. Grieve the loss of the graduation, the engagement, the wedding, the grandchild, the vacations . . . Look at any UNRESOLVED grief that you may have with your loved one. Unresolved grief might be anger, blame or guilt that you still carry associated with your loved one and his or her death. I used to teach these concepts at my healing center, and I would lead the participants through the steps to do this work. I know it's hard. It hurts. Quite frankly, it completely sucks. I get it. But it is such healing work. Please believe me when I tell you that if you don't feel your grief now, it will haunt you for the rest of your life— somehow, someway. It will lay hidden, quiet, furtive, until sooner or later it will explode. Or, worse yet, you live out your life with anger, bitterness, hatred, resentment. Or, in some cases, you choose to succumb to suicidal thoughts.

You must say yes to suffering before you can transcend it. How powerful is that statement? Saying yes to suffering is *conscious suffering*. Choose to suffer; choose to feel your pain. Choose to cry and scream and kick the floor. Take a conscious approach to your own healing. When you do, transformation awaits.

We must say yes to our suffering. We must allow it—all of it. Every tear, every angry thought, every single ounce of guilt and blame. We must acknowledge it, feel it, and then release it. That sets us on the pathway toward healing. That sets us on the pathway toward acceptance.

CHAPTER ELEVEN

The MomChild Reunion

In the spring of 2010, I attended the Sun Valley Wellness Festival. This annual event is a lovely festival with all types of new age or spiritual businesses on hand selling their crafts, jewelry, and services. I went with my friend Jill Renee Feeler, who is now a leading spiritual teacher and intuitive. Jill had a small booth at the festival and I went to support and assist her.

During a break, as I was roaming the exhibit hall, I noticed a banner that read "MomChild Reunion" at the end of a long row of booths. I saw a man there, and a few pieces of literature on the table. That was all. Very plain—nothing shiny or fancy to draw you in. I shied away from the booth, intent on spending my time at more interesting displays: Discover your Soul Purpose, See Your Aura Colors, Reflexology—fun things like that. That little voice in my head (you know the one) kept telling me to go talk to the man at the booth. I pointedly ignored the voice and avoided the booth again, instead venturing around the corner and into a conversation with a lovely woman who provided Soul Purpose readings based on your fingerprints. (I did actually purchase that reading which was quite phenomenal.) Yet still the little voice persisted. Having learned that the voice will not be quieted when it has something important to say, I walked over to the booth. Our conversation went something like this:

me: Hi. I'm not sure why I'm here but . . .

man: Hi, how are you today?

me: I'm fine, thank you. What do you do?

man: My name is Steve Baldwin and my wife, Sally Baldwin, and I hold a retreat for mothers who have lost a child.

me: (surprised) Oh! Well, I have lost a child.

man: Really? Well, if you'd like to sign up, we will send you some information.

Steve and I chatted for a little bit. I learned that his wife, Sally, was a gifted and well-known channeler who had written numerous books. The MomChild Reunion was a sponsored event that she and Steve put all their energy into. This was their second year of holding the retreat. As promised, Steve sent me the application and I applied. I later discovered there were over one-hundred applicants and only seven of us were chosen to attend. Virtually all of our expenses (with the exception of my gas driving from Boise to Sun Valley) were paid by a beautiful and generous woman who sponsored the entire event—airfare, hotel rooms, meals—truly amazing. Almost all of the applicants had heard about the retreat from a website and chat room for grieving parents that I was not a part of. Nothing short of absolute divine intervention placed me in the right place at the right time to meet Steve and to hear about the MomChild Reunion opportunity. I am so glad that I listened to my inner voice and approached Steve Baldwin that day. Later, Sally told me that Bryan literally would not leave her alone during the selection process. *"Pick my mom, pick my mom, you HAVE to pick my mom,"* he told her daily, until she replied, "Bryan your mom is in!" That wasn't the first or the last time that Bryan was pretty pushy with a medium to get what he wanted!

The workshop was a three-and-a-half-day event in Sun Valley, Idaho in October 2010. Our group consisted of myself and six other moms from Oregon, Illinois, Ohio, Georgia, New Zealand, and England. Our children's death dates ranged from only a few months prior to the retreat to the span of two and a half years prior. For me it had been just over two years since Bryan had died. While I had already been dabbling in the spiritual world, the Baldwins opened my eyes to a set of healing tools that further prepared me to help myself and others. Sally and her team taught us about reiki, crystals, massage, spirit animals, HeartMath Technology,

Emotional Freedom Technique, the Enneagram Personality Diagram (information that helped us understand ourselves and our children's personalities), the Michael Teachings, and even a more traditional grief recovery exercise.

It was a powerful weekend absolutely jam-packed with information. We all had a bit of sensory overload I think, by the end of it. One night we gathered in one of our beautiful hotel rooms at the Sun Valley Resort and started a huge pillow fight. We laughed and rolled around on the beds and the floor, just to unwind and temper our sadness a bit. We remarked at the time, "If people could see us now they wouldn't believe that we are all grieving mothers, they would think we are crazy." We WERE crazy—crazy with love for Sally and Steve, for each other, and of course for our children who were developing these new relationships with us. We would walk along the gorgeous grounds of the resort and breathe in the mountain air. We ate fabulous food and laughed some more. For some of our group, those were the first laughs in a long time.

That retreat reopened my heart, gave me renewed purpose and catapulted me forward in my healing. By coming together as a group to share our stories, feel our pain, and learn the tools that would help us heal, the seven of us became forever bonded. We are called The Sun Valley Moms and we hold regular reunions to this day.

Above all else, though, Sally taught us how to communicate with our children. She gifted each of us a beautiful crystal pendulum and an alphabet wheel, teaching us a method by which we could talk to our kids. We practiced as a group and Sally helped us decipher the broken messages we were receiving. Letter by letter, word by word, we would watch the pendulum spell out messages. Similar to a Ouija board, Spirit's energy moves the pendulum and pauses at letters on the wheel to spell out a message. It was fascinating, although most of us didn't trust the process right away. None of us were frightened; there was absolutely no negativity attached to the practice at all. However, we were taught to always ground ourselves and ask for God's protection before engaging in any form of spirit communication.

For me, this form of channeling opened the door to communicate directly with Bryan. I never did completely trust the pendulum because I couldn't shake the notion that my own energy might somehow influence the movement of the crystal. However, I do feel that learning how to use this type of communication tool was a BIG step forward in my intuitive and telepathic communications with Bryan.

Be open to everything. Whatever process resonates with you, trust it. Try to feel into the experience with your heart rather than your head. It doesn't have to make sense, and it may never make sense intellectually. Feel it in all that you do. Every step you take creates a path. If you question everything, you hold the energy hostage to your understanding—let go. Have the willingness to be open and explore, even those things you don't understand.

Chapter Twelve

More of Sally Baldwin's Legacy

One of the most important understandings I gained from Sally was that I needed to be open to receiving Bryan AS HE IS NOW, not as the sandy-haired boy that I had birthed and nurtured for twenty-three years, because his physical presence was indeed gone. She taught me to embrace Bryan as the soul being that he is now—sure, he has lost his physical form, but he is still smart and funny and a little sarcastic; he is still determined and creative and loving.

This is such a difficult concept for many grieving parents. We want our children back—exactly as they were. We want to hug them and kiss them and turn around to see them next to us. We want to touch their hair, their face, their fingers and toes. We don't want to let that go, just like there is a part of us that doesn't want to stop grieving them at all. Because if we stop grieving the loss of their physicality, we stop grieving THEM, and we will have betrayed them.

This is one of the biggest misguided beliefs that we as grieving parents all seem to experience, and probably most grieving people in general have felt this way—if we heal from our grief, we will have betrayed our loved one. So, we subconsciously choose NOT to heal because we don't want to abandon our beloved. When I voiced that concern to Sally at the conclusion of our first evening together, this is what she said:

> If you are going to connect and know your children as they are, and if you are going to find that connection in a deep and abiding way with who they are, and if you are going to take that step as the souls that you are, to lead with your spirit and not your physicality of ego, body, and mind, then YES you must seek the portal that says I want to know you NOW.

> Now when you put that forth, you are not forgetting, you are not ignoring, you are not pushing away who they were, these beautiful beings, these spirits of light in your life as your children, and yet you are accepting that they can be more than that, and you are putting yourselves in the position of saying, "I can carry those recollections, those memories, and the dear feelings they bring up in me as the mother of this child." But simultaneously you can also use it as a platform to spring into saying, "I want to know you now. I want to be able to fill some of the space that the pain is holding with who you are in your current state of being so that you and I can become comfortable,

can become acquainted, we can know each other in a way that goes beyond and surpasses what we were about as mother and son, or mother and daughter."

That's the promise that has brought you here, as much as you have expressed the pain of it, the promise is that you are now ready to say, "If I am to connect with you I want it to be more than just what I remember, I want to take you right now in the moment of who you are and I want to commune, I want to find you. I want a sense of who you are." But that doesn't mean you give up the dearness and the importance and even the painfulness of what you and they were about on the earth. You are physical, you hold onto that in as many different ways as can be helpful to you. But when it steps out of helpfulness and it becomes a tool to just simply survive, pushes the door closed, and does not let your children come forward as the wondrous immortal souls they are, then you are not helping yourself or them or anyone else. And every one of you is capable of this. You are capable of discernment and we are joining with you.

Heartbreakingly, Sally passed away in 2012 from heart disease. She and Steve hosted one more MomChild Reunion in 2011 but there were to be no more. She is sorely missed by all who knew her, and especially by the Moms who were fortunate enough to be blessed by her, and whose lives she dramatically changed.

Seek out your loved ones as they are now. Let go of any limiting beliefs you may hold about what heaven is or is not, or about what we as souls do or don't have or do or don't look like when we die. Trust that your beloveds carry the same love for you, even greater, than before they died. Nothing has really changed, except their physical bodies are gone. The rest of them lives on and is waiting for you. There is no betrayal here, simply acceptance. And acceptance brings peace.

Chapter Thirteen
Grief Surges

Throughout our journey toward healing we may find that, unexpectedly and frequently, like ocean waves that tumultuously surge against a rocky shoreline, our emotions continue to roll over us, bringing back the pain of our grief as if we're experiencing the event that triggered our grief all over again. I call these *Grief Surges*—those out-of-the-blue emotional tailspins that can send us spiraling downward with no forethought and no warning. Ah, if only we could protect ourselves from grief surges!

One morning while driving to work I passed a blonde-haired little boy waiting at the bus stop. He was probably six or seven years old and was wearing a blue shirt and carrying a red backpack just like Bryan did on his first day of first grade. I immediately spiraled down into a grief surge that was so intense I had to pull over to the side of the road. So many memories of my little tow-headed Bryan doing the same, waiting at the bus stop, excited for the new adventures he would experience that day.

Sometimes we can predict when a grief surge might occur. Birthdays, holidays, or revisiting places where we shared fond memories with our loved ones who have passed are certainly triggers. But more often than not, like seeing the little boy at the bus stop, they just happen. I found I could be in quite a good mood, not particularly thinking about my son at a particular moment, and then it would hit me. I would instantly be transported back to a moment in time on or around that fateful day, and immediately I would be panicked and racked with fresh pain over losing him.

If I was lucky, the grief surge would only last a few minutes. But sometimes they lasted for days, weeks or much longer. Over the first year and a half after Bryan's passing, the surges were non-stop. One rolled right into the next and there was no relief whatsoever. Miraculously, over time, they started to subside, and I found I could breathe again—until the next one hit.

The longest single surge I remember having started right after Thanksgiving a few years after Bryan passed. I spiraled down, down, down . . . and I couldn't find the light anymore. I didn't realize I was in a grief surge; I just knew that I was angry, and sad, and depressed. It wasn't until the following New Year's Day that I finally started to swim back up from the depths of my pain, and even then it took many messages from Spirit and loving friends (and strangers also) before I started feeling a little better.

Grief surges are serious. We all have had them. We can't always predict when one is going to hit, and we usually don't recognize we are in them until they have passed. How we react to these grief surges can determine whether or not we will allow them to control us, or if we shall choose to control them. What can we do? How can we find our way out of the intensity of these surges? Well, read on. I can share with you some things that worked for me. Maybe they will work for you also.

The waves of grief are just that—waves. They swell and they recede. In the beginning weeks and months, sometimes years of grief, the waves can be constant—but they do lessen over time. If we never loved, we would never grieve. That same love that you are now grieving is what will set you free. You must allow the waves of grief in order to continue healing, but there are tools you can use to help get you through them.

Chapter Fourteen

Meditation

Breathe in, breathe out, focus on your breath. When your brain starts busily thinking, return your attention to your breath. Good job, you're meditating! This is one of the most effective ways that I know of to ease the panic of a grief surge, and even to help prevent the onset of one, with a regular meditation practice.

In November 2009 I experienced a very moving and profound meditation. I was still fairly new to the practice and began with prayer. I prayed for peace and love, and for the anger in me to be removed. Things like that. Then I started crying, deep painful crying, for a long time. Then I tried to connect with Bryan directly. I held tightly to a picture of him. In my mind's eye, I saw his face floating around me, and felt like he was trying to reach me and maybe take me somewhere, but I couldn't quite connect. Then I was just floating for a long time, in a beautiful peaceful place. There was a lot of white light and . . . I can't even describe it . . . it was beautiful. I didn't notice any colors, just a lot of brilliant white and heavenly-type images. Then I (telepathically) heard someone instructing me to pick up my notebook, there was a message for me. I didn't want to . . . told this messenger I didn't want to . . . wanted to stay in this beautiful peaceful state/place. Then I heard, *"NOW, PLEASE."* I sighed and opened my eyes (which by the way was very difficult to do because my tears had glued them shut) and picked up my notebook. This is what I was told:

"We want you to understand that this was a choice you made when you were here. Your capacity to love is endless and you will feel it again in your life. Bryan knew that you could support him like no other. We know living with his physical death is more difficult than you thought it would be. Life is often difficult which is why some of us choose to stay here. Time is not relevant. You will see Bryan again, sooner than you think, and it will be glorious! He is glorious, and he is waiting for that day also. In the meantime, we want you to focus on the self, the journey, and prepare yourself. For the day is coming near that all hearts must choose. Choose love or choose fear. You and your friends are discovering the joy of pure love—that state of being that is pure bliss when you are filled with God, and unconditional love for all matter and all beings. Bryan is but one of those beautiful beings. Expand your love to include everyone. We know it is difficult. We know you miss him so. You will see him as you remember him, but your soul knows much more. You can remember, if you believe in yourself. The grief you feel is good because you must do this. Do not be so hard on yourself. We hear you. We are here to help you."

Wow! This was my first experience with what is known as automatic writing. There are different ways to receive messages from Spirit. One way is through channeling the information—Spirit speaks through one of the "clairs" that we learned about in Chapter Nine—clairvoyance, clairaudience, clairsentience and claircognizance. Another way to receive messages from Spirit is through Automatic Writing, which is where you allow Spirit to create or guide the words that you write. Also considered a psychic gift, this is one of the easiest types of psychic communication abilities to develop. Simply put, it involves allowing Spirit, or sometimes your higher self, to simply flow through you. You write without thinking, in fact I usually don't remember the words I've written while automatic writing. Typically, I am prompted by Spirit to write—that is to say I have an overwhelming knowingness that a message is ready to be sent, as I described above. The words flow very quickly, smoothly, without any forethought or consideration on my part. When my hand stops writing, I know the communication is finished. As a writer, this is one of my favorite ways to receive Spirit communication! Automatic writing may be done using a computer, or by handwriting (I've done both). The poem "Believe" in Chapter Nineteen was automatic writing that Bryan nudged me to open up and receive.

I don't know who was speaking to me that day. Maybe it was God, maybe it was Angels, maybe it was my Spirit Guides. It doesn't really matter. What matters is that I trusted that the message came from a divine source, and it calmed me immensely.

When I first began to meditate I used free guided recordings to help me. Usually these were focused meditations with the sole purpose of meeting and talking with my beloved son again. In the beginning I would lie on my bed and close my eyes. I had an iPod speaker next to my bed and I would alternate between one or two different recordings that I had downloaded. In the stillness of my mind I would follow the narrator out of my chair and through the door and over the bridge, and there I would wait expectantly. But always, before Bryan would appear, my tears would flow so hard that I would have to stop. The pain of losing him was so great and painful still that I couldn't see him in this non-physical form. But I wouldn't give up. I kept trying, again and again. Finally, one day, I saw him approaching me through the fog. He walked up to me and hugged me and we just held each other for what seemed like a very long time. His hug was so loving, so tender, so beautiful. I knew it was real and I basked in his love as it washed over me.

Another time I experienced a short but very intense meditation and journaled this about it: *I felt Bryan with me. I felt his energy body—it seemed to be about twenty-four inches wide. I felt warmth; tingling, intense sensations. I remembered him exactly as he was; how he walked and talked while in his earthly body. I thought about my own soul being and instantly I was pulled upward . . . up, up, up in a beam of white light. I saw an energy body of swirling colors . . .*

reds, oranges, and yellows. Me? Bryan? Then I saw a paintbrush with multiple colors swirled together—he was trying to tell me something about the swirl of many colors but I couldn't grasp his meaning. But I did get this message: He wants me to NOT STOP FEELING in regard to his passing. I have been pushing it down—not feeling it. If I don't FEEL him and my feelings for him, I can't project my love and find him in that love. It's like out of sight/out of mind . . . out of feeling/out of connectedness. Don't stop feeling. Through sorrow we find unconditional love. Through sorrow we find joy.

There is no right or wrong way to meditate. The point is to try and quiet the mind and find the peaceful center of your being. There are a wide variety of meditation options available: both guided and unguided meditations, mindfulness, breath awareness, mantra, transcendental—even simple soothing music works. What is successful for one person is not successful for all. Try a meditation app, like Insight or Headspace, to help you get started and choose what works for you. Don't be afraid to seek out your loved one in your meditation. Focus your attention on your heart and summon up an image of your loved one. Stay in your heart, and FEEL the love being exchanged between the two of you. Your loved one will respond with all the love and compassion and energy you could ask for! As a tool to help ease a grief surge, meditation can be very powerful.

Spirit is infinitely committed to you. Spirit holds unconditional, abundant and joyous love for each and every one of us on this earth. Spirit's everlasting promise is to support, honor and assist us. Spirit is so proud of our growth and our expansion, and ecstatically rejoices when we connect with Spirit on a conscious level. Spirit is waiting for your call! Meditation is a way to place that call.

CHAPTER FIFTEEN

Alternative Healing

*T*he State of California extended a very generous offer of free grief counseling for Bryan's immediate family. I was not naturally a fan of traditional counseling but decided to give it a try. Well, actually, my husband convinced me to give it a try. Poor guy, he just wasn't sure how to help me, but he never gave up on me. Thank the good Lord for that. And, after all, it WAS free…

So, I called around and found a therapist who agreed to bill the State of California for our sessions. The first time I went, I was so scared my whole body shook. On one hand I've always been kind of an open book, but I also am very private about deeply emotional things, and I definitely don't like to lose control in front of anyone. Of course, she wanted me to tell her all about how Bryan had died which I couldn't do without crying uncontrollably. I saw her three times and each visit I cried and cried, but never felt better. So, while she was very nice and I'm sure she was an excellent therapist, I felt as though her intention each week was just to make me cry. Well, I did plenty of that on my own; I didn't need her help!

This rejection of traditional grief counseling furthered my desire to seek other forms of healing. For example, I had been introduced to the Reiki session during the MomChild Reunion. That treatment, a form of energy healing, had a profound effect on me. I lay on a massage table, fully clothed, with a light blanket covering me and a bolster under my knees for comfort. The Reiki practitioner was seated in a chair at the head of the table. She silently said a prayer, waved her hands around my head, then placed them on my forehead. Immediately I started to drift away, swirling dots of light filling my consciousness as I drifted deeper and deeper into a trance-like state. As she moved her hands to various positions on my body, I became aware of being inside of a beautiful, translucent, quartz crystal. I was embodied in it, similar to a butterfly that is encased in its chrysalis. The brilliance of the light radiating around me was so calming and so soothing. I floated in its majesty for what seemed a very long time. Eventually, the practitioner tapped my feet and began talking softly to me, calling me back into my body. Afterward, I felt as if healing had occurred. Not that my grief had been removed from me, but I had a new calmness, a new awareness that all would be well. I felt cleansed, rejuvenated, re-energized.

I returned home and shared my amazing experience with my friend Jill. We both wanted to learn more, so after researching various other forms of energy healing, we decided to take a beginner course in Pranic Healing. We learned the basic techniques used to scan, cleanse, and seal the body's energy fields. The technique is completely hands-off and can be done with the person lying down or standing. One of my favorite discoveries related to this practice is the *Om Namo Parabrahman Om* meditation. This guided meditation is so beautiful, so loving, so ethereal. One time while deeply immersed in the energies of it, I became aware that I was sitting at the feet of God. I have never felt such love! Tears streamed down my face as I felt His love wash over me. It was with deep regret that I heard the narrator's voice calling me back into my body.

Reiki is a Japanese healing art that involves laying hands on the body to comfort and relieve pain and promote well-being. Like Pranic Healing, Reiki heals on all levels—physical, mental, emotional and spiritual, and helps return the body to its natural perfect state. After my initial Reiki experience at the MomChild Reunion, and after exploring Pranic Healing, I decided Reiki was the modality I wanted to practice. I discovered that there was (and still is) a Reiki Center in Boise so I signed up for the workshop that would certify me in Level I Reiki. I later continued on with my Level II certification. Reiki I allows you to practice Reiki on yourself, Reiki II allows you to use the practice on other people. A Reiki master, which I did not pursue, allows a practitioner to then teach Reiki to others. Over a period of about five years, I shared my healing practice with many people. As is the case with most Reiki practitioners, I developed my own unique process and found that a combination of Reiki and Pranic Healing were very powerful in my sessions. Each session was unique and healing in its own way, as much for me as for my clients. Reiki energy is so calming, so healing, so truthful. There is a vulnerability to opening yourself to Divine energy, letting it flow through you as it needs to, locating your areas of weakness and directing its strengths there. Most people leave a Reiki session feeling very relaxed, as if they'd just received a massage. Reiki works on a deep level throughout the body's energy system and will continue to flow through you for days following a session.

Pranic Healing and Reiki are just two of many different forms or modifications of alternative energy healing. Though they use different techniques, they use the same source of energy to heal. That source of energy is God, the Creator, the Divine, Heavenly Father or Mother. I use the name God but please use whatever resonates with you.

Energy healing embodies the belief that the human body can heal itself by protecting the physical body through cleansing of the aura, and that if disease is removed from our auric field then disease will not manifest in one's physical body.

ReikiCoachingTherapy.com describes it like this: "Our aura or auric field contains information about our life such as our emotional and mental thoughts, beliefs and memories. The chakras, which are the seven wheels of spinning energy where universal life flows up and down the body, connecting the physical to the spiritual, also have an effect on the aura and can create changes in the color and shape of our aura. No two auras are exactly the same as we are constantly shifting our vibrations due to changes in our thought patterns. When we are low in energy and feeling down, our aura naturally shrinks to reflect this. When we are upbeat and happy our aura naturally expands, radiating outward."

The different layers of the aura that protect the physical body (listed from the closest layer to the physical body to the furthest) are the Etheric Layer which relates to the physical condition of the body; the Emotional Layer which holds all our emotions, feelings and sensitivity such as joy, sorrow, love and hate; the Mental Layer which contains our mental thought processes such as rules, regulations, judgement and discipline; the Astral Layer which is the bridge between the lower vibrations of the physical plane and the higher vibrations of the spiritual; the Etheric Template which represents the blueprint of the physical body and looks much like the negative of a photograph; the Celestial/Causal Layer which is where your spiritual connection begins; and the Spiritual Layer which protects all the other layers and vibrates at the highest frequency.

So, simply put, in most forms of energy healing the practitioner is cleansing and smoothing out these different auric layers and chakras, using God's divine white light and energy to guide them. It is that divine white light and energy that is transmitted through the practitioner's hands and into the body of the person on the table. Practitioners usually do charge money for a healing session, the average at the time of this writing runs $50-$100 per session, but there are some folks who provide Reiki for no charge—check your local holistic healing schools or university programs.

Also, don't underestimate the power of simple body movement

and massage therapy! My body felt so heavy and sluggish most of the time in the first five years of my journey. I signed up for yoga lessons, but I couldn't even get through one class without crying. That's when I became acutely aware that grief was storing itself in my muscles. As my body moved, the grief energy would become unlocked and would rise to the surface. I would leave class feeling drained on many levels, partly because there was important "work" taking place in my healing journey. Receiving massage therapy in addition to doing some form of regular body movement activity would be icing on the cake, because a good massage therapist will help you move that unstuck energy out of your body.

It doesn't end there, though. Throughout this journey I've experienced many forms of healing from so many gifted healers. Each one was brought into my life just when I needed them most. I believe that Bryan, my God and my Spirit team guided me toward each and every one of them—Reiki, massage, crystal therapy healing, acupuncture, essential oil remedies—they all served a purpose in my healing at the times that I needed them. When I first became a spiritual seeker, I was concerned about what my family and friends would think of me and these new "woo woo" practices that I was adopting. But while a lot of the new things I was learning admittedly seemed a little weird to me and others, I kept on trying new and different modalities and approaches to healing. I was determined to find Bryan, and to find peace within myself. Besides, none of it was weird to the cultures who have been practicing these healing methods for eons. And because I was willing to try them, I found they worked!

Another method for healing can be found through attending a grief support group that resonates with you. There are numerous good bereavement groups. The Helping Parents Heal (HPH) organization was the one that I chose, because what I discovered after researching the different options, was a very fundamental difference between HPH and other groups.

While HPH is a support group for parents who have a child who passed, they go beyond traditional bereavement groups by offering an open discussion of spiritual experiences and evidence for the afterlife, in a non-dogmatic way. As this philosophy completely mirrored my own beliefs and journey, I contacted the President and Co-Founder, Elizabeth Boisson, and, after learning there were not any meetings in Boise at that time, offered to host a local Boise chapter. Our group of parents gathered weekly to talk about our healing and learn about alternative methods just like the ones I've mentioned in this book: meditation, crystal healing, emotional freedom technique, mediumship and many others. Much, much healing took place during those meetings, and yes, lots of tears were also shed. But for every tear that was shed, we opened ourselves up even more to the glorious possibility of living a life with our child(ren) still present—not gone! During the time that I facilitated our group, I formed deep friendships with other grieving parents in my community. Currently I serve as a Caring Listener for Helping Parents Heal, which is a non-profit organization.

Explore! Be a seeker outside of traditional medicine and traditional therapies. Be conscious with your healing and be mindful of what makes you feel good and what doesn't. If it doesn't make you feel good, don't be afraid to walk away.

Chapter Sixteen
The Miracles of Nature

Have you ever stopped to appreciate the amazing synchronicities of our existence? Have you ever opened your eyes and ears to be in tune with God and with nature? It's truly amazing! While on this journey I have learned to open my eyes and to really SEE what is happening around me, and to FEEL the love and guidance being sent to me.

And I learned how much nature really is God's true medicine. I love to walk outdoors when I am experiencing deep grief surges. Being outside and feeling the crisp air on my skin makes me feel alive again. Even in my darkest hours I can still manage to find joy in the wonderment of this earth and all her beauty. And it's free therapy!

There's nothing like activating our body's endorphins to lift our energy and our mood and bring us some clarity of thought. Even if you can only summon up enough energy to walk for 10 minutes, just do it! Start with what you can do and gradually add distance to your routine. Hiking is my solace. In Boise we are so fortunate to be surrounded by beautiful foothills that contain miles and miles of hiking trails. I am able to hear Bryan more clearly while I'm hiking; I never listen to music because I want to hear him. I also love listening to my feet hit the dirt and listening to the birds and the other sounds around me. I feel close to God and close to Bryan when I'm on the trail. Sometimes I feel desperate for the sound of water; on those days I walk along our greenbelt that runs adjacent to the Boise River. And some days when I don't have the energy to drive anywhere, I just walk in my neighborhood or up and down my dirt lane.

My good friend Terry and I used to hike together frequently in the first seven or eight years after Bryan's death. We would hike for miles—I would talk, she would listen. As Terry is a devout Christian, I expected her to struggle to understand my enthusiasm and experiences regarding my newfound spirituality and the afterlife. But instead of rejecting me or trying to force me to change my beliefs, she instead looked for similarities between my beliefs and hers. I realized later that I was evolving as our conversations progressed; she helped me firm up my thoughts and put some of my beliefs into words. I can't overestimate the importance of having someone in your life that you can talk with, be honest with, be vulnerable with. While I have so many loving people in my support system, Terry was "my person" that I discussed spiritual concepts with and I'm eternally grateful to her and for her.

Bryan frequently joins me on solitary hikes and walks. Just weeks before this writing, I was taking a quick hike before a morning appointment. I had been ill with severe allergies and was feeling weak and out of shape. Even so, I took what I considered the "hard way up" on that morning, which meant that the climb up the mountain was less steep but longer and more gradual—more taxing for me, actually. Once I reached the summit, I realized I was going to run out of time, so I started to run on the backside, which was all downhill. Now, I am not a runner! Never have been. I ran over one mile all the way down that mountain without any problems, almost like I was running on a cloud. When I got to my car I thought, Wow, that was pretty cool! I actually ran down that whole mountain. Immediately I heard Bryan talking to me, explaining that he helped to carry me down the mountain, to rebuild my confidence and to prove to me that I am strong. I was so grateful to him for explaining that to me, and so excited to have that experience and exchange with him.

Walking, hiking, running, biking—whatever outside activity it is that you enjoy, is excellent medicine for the soul, the body, and the mind. But even just sitting outside in nature is good for you as well. I recall one Sunday where I had an amazing and unexpected visit from Bryan as I was resting in my hammock in the backyard, after planting some new perennials in my garden. Listening to the birds and the breeze, I was suddenly filled with what I call the "Bryan Hug"—that intense whoosh of energy that fills my entire being, that is sweetly reminiscent of him, and which is simply overflowing with love. This wave lingered for a while, calming me as I felt it travel through me and around me. I held on to it as long as I could, talking to him and sending him waves of my own love in return. I love my Bryan hugs!

Nature feeds the soul. It is necessary and vital to knowing who you are. When in nature, we can get a glimpse into our souls, a glimmer of truth into our reasons for being, a hint of understanding into the purpose behind our circumstances. The whisper of God is in the air, your loved one is by your side, and the beauty of nature surrounding you offers peace and calming.

Chapter Seventeen

Prayer and Gratitude

I know you've heard this a thousand times or more, but I can't impress upon you enough the power of Prayer and Gratitude. Remembering to be grateful every day for whatever you can find to be grateful for is so important. Your family, friends, the home you live in, the food on your table, your pet, the clothes on your back— anything! When we remember what we are grateful for then life doesn't seem quite so full of despair. If we can find just ONE thing that we are grateful for, then we have a spark of hope. When we have hope, we lessen the intensity of the pain we are experiencing.

Here's what you can do. Write down three things that you are grateful for every morning right after your feet hit the floor. Follow that up with a short prayer or meditation and FEEL the gratitude in your heart and in your belly. That gratitude will generate further things to be grateful for. The universe will give you exactly what you ask for. My experience has shown me that my mind grows by what it feeds on. If I focus my energy on "poor me" then I'll receive more things to feel bad about. But if I focus my energy on "lucky me," I will receive more things to be grateful for. It really is that simple.

In addition to writing down three things that you are grateful for each morning, you can also list three positive affirmations for yourself. Affirmations can be empowering statements such as "I am healing," "I am physically strong," "I am healthy," "I am intuitive"—whatever you WANT for yourself to be true, write it down. Put an end to the negative conversations that you have with yourself. This is the first step toward finding self-love. This is YOU reclaiming your power. Own it. Become the person you want to be. It starts with gratitude.

Prayer is simply the single most powerful way I know of to calm my entire being. Prayer is the act of deliberately communicating with your version of your God or Higher Power. As my niece Mandy so beautifully stated, "Prayer is how we feel God's love."

I am so very grateful to be Bryan's mom. I wouldn't trade one moment of the twenty-three years and almost five months I had with him, even knowing what I know now about how his physical life would end. I know you feel the same about your beloved. If you can't feel anything else, feel that. Feel into how grateful you are for your beloved and build from there.

With gratitude in our hearts, we can find happiness with what we have, and we find we can have hope for the future. Those little things that we let bother us don't seem as important. Love becomes heartfelt, and peace becomes attainable. Invite in that which you want more of in your life.

Chapter Eighteen

Finding Joy

Grief is a journey. A zigzagging, upward climbing, downward spiraling, yo-yo of a journey. Two steps forward, three steps back. Three steps forward, one step back. I continued in this way over the first six or seven years after Bryan died. I kept on seeking, exploring, trying new things, trying to understand how and why this had happened to us, to Bryan. And what I finally faced is this—after everything I had learned, after all of the miracles, and after all of the wonderful, most amazing connections I experienced with Bryan—still there was THE PAIN. I was stuck in my story of pain. Would I ever find joy again?

The initial pain was all about HOW my son died—my son was murdered. Not to say that murder is more difficult to overcome than grief associated with accidents, illness or suicide: no loss is greater than another. It is important that we never compare our loss to another's because we cannot know the depths of their love, or the depths of the pain that they carry in their hearts. But with murder, there is such an extreme feeling of unfairness. I was so angry about it that the healing and the love being offered to me couldn't get through. It was easy to allow murder to justify my anger and my grief and my bitterness, because someone else did something bad, something deadly, to my child. The same can be said when it's an accident or a disease that takes our loved one from us. Suicide adds even another layer of grief and anger – and blame. So what do we do with this?

The truth is, it doesn't really matter HOW our beloveds left us. In the big scheme of things, they are gone, and we are still here. We can find them again, as you are learning, but we simply must set aside our stories of the how and the why of their deaths. If we want to find our loved one where they are now, we have to dig out of that hole and accept that "what is, is." And set our sights on "What now?" "Where are you?" "How can I find you?" We cannot change the past, and we cannot affect the future if we don't act in the present. Grieve—yes. Tell your story as long as you need to— yes. But know that when you're ready to set your story aside, you will be opening the door to allow your healing in on a deeper level, and to allowing your loved one to communicate with you much more easily and regularly.

Over time, finding joy became my new obsession. I used to obsess about whether or not some girl out there in the world had birthed Bryan's child and how I might find them—crazy, right? I even wrote an email to a female friend of Bryan's that I believe he dated once or twice in the weeks preceding his death, and actually asked her if maybe she were pregnant. I fantasized for years that one day my doorbell would ring and there before me would be Bryan's child. "Hi Grandma," he or she would say, and I would fall to my knees with joy. Or I would obsess about what my soul purpose was—in the spiritual world where I live, soul purpose means the work we came here to do. I spent much time and, yes, money getting readings and taking courses and ordering astrological charts—all to find out what my true purpose was after losing my son.

But eventually I came around to joy. The lack of continuous, free-flowing joy in my life made me feel like a fake, pretending to be healed so that others would be more comfortable. Could I find joy again? Lo and behold, I was led to yet another great teacher, Tom Zuba. Tom is the author of two wonderful books on grief. He lives with the deaths of two beloved children and his lovely wife. I had become familiar with his work through social media. His words of wisdom always brought me peace, and his journey seemed to mirror my own. So, I reached out to Tom one day. "Can you teach me how to find joy?" I asked, and he replied, "Yes." When the student is ready, the teacher appears.

Tom teaches to give yourself *Permission to Mourn*, which is also the title of his first book. But he also taught me that before I could find joy, I needed to *grieve the person I was before Bryan died.*

I needed to grieve her, and all of the hopes and dreams that she had for herself and for her son. Oh. My. This was a big deal. Lots more tears. Lots more screams. Lots more begging of God to please show me the way—help me to understand. I needed to let her go. All of those dreams I'd carried since before Bryan was born—I needed to let them go. All of them. They were not to be. Not this time, not this life.

One day my husband told me in frustration, "Paige, you didn't die. Bryan died." Ouch. That hurt! We were standing outside in the driveway and my immediate reaction was anger. How dare he say such a thing to me! Upon reflection, though, I understood what he meant. It was time for me to start living again. It was time for me to start walking the walk, not just talking the talk. I think that was when I really, truly woke up from my nightmare. That was when I saw how much other people in my life needed me still.

Spirit had actually sent me a similar message as early as 2009, as Dwaine and I were eating breakfast while attending a motorcycle rally in Elko, Nevada. In the middle of our meal I heard *"pay attention to the living"* loudly inside my head. I don't recall what he and I had been discussing, but I remember the force with which those words were delivered to me, telepathically. A few months after receiving that message, I asked Jade if I could start babysitting our little granddaughter Tayler on Fridays. She was barely one year old at the time, and I tell you, that girl became such a huge part of my healing, just by letting me love her, play with her, and care for her. Two years later our granddaughter Ryenn joined our "Gana and Papa Day" tradition, followed by sweet Maddyn four years later. Our granddaughter Hadley lives out of state but believe me it's pure joy (and sometimes chaos) when we are all together!

But back to that day with Dwaine. . . . It became so clear to me then—Did I REALLY want to live, or did I REALLY want to die? Even though I had chosen not to take the path of suicide on that road to the lake so many years before, still I wondered. Did I REALLY want to live? Because as long as there was any part of me silently choosing death, then joy would remain elusive. Did I want to live? Or did I want to die? I decided I wanted to live. I said the words out loud. "I WANT TO LIVE. I CHOOSE LIFE."

Grief is so selfish, and deservedly so. I was so selfish in my grief I had forgotten that others were grieving Bryan also. My husband, my stepchildren, Bryan's father and his family, Bryan's friends, my friends. We all were grieving the loss of that very remarkable and exceptional young man. But they were all also grieving the loss of ME, the loss of their wife, stepmom, grandmother, sister, and friend. I'm so grateful to my husband for speaking those words to me that day. It was time for me to live again. It was time for me to love again.

It is okay to be selfish in your grief, how could you not be? It is important to allow yourself the time you need on your unique journey to tell your story and feel your pain and express your anger. But do not forsake yourself, do not give up your desire to laugh, to be happy, to be joyful. Keep reaching for the fullness of a joy-filled life—find joy in all that you can—in a child's laugh, in a loved one's embrace, in the warmth of a fire. Carry that joy in your heart and invite more joy in every day.

CHAPTER NINETEEN
Choose to Believe

*B*ryan and God blessed us with miracle after miracle—so many signs that our son was still present and a part of our lives. And yet still, years into my healing journey, I had doubts that would continue to creep in occasionally, unsolicited but present nonetheless. Was it *really* Bryan? Was he *really* communicating with us? My mental mind didn't understand it. I wasn't one-hundred percent sure I truly believed any of it. I had nagging fears and doubts that kept me distant from God and prevented me from fully connecting with my son.

I was so tired of doubting. No matter how many amazing signs Bryan sent us, no matter how many readings I received from reputable mediums, no matter how many times my own higher self nudged me and spoke to me . . . still doubt would raise its ugly head from time to time. It was holding me back, keeping me down, literally choking me, preventing me from healing and moving forward.

One day, something truly miraculous happened. I heard these words in meditation: CHOOSE TO BELIEVE. Choose to believe that it is all real—my son's voice, the messages, the signs, the miracles. I understood that until I really DID believe, I could simply CHOOSE to believe. *And that would be enough. For now.* That was a critical moment in time for me.

After I made the decision to "choose to believe" everything broke wide open for me. Over time I realized that I no longer needed proof of anything! I wasn't "choosing to believe" anymore—I truly DID believe. My heart had been opened and there was no turning back.

Bryan and I wrote about this in an automatic writing session we did together in December 2014. It is titled "Believe." The credit for these words belongs to Bryan—he wrote through me so fast and so clearly…I was merely his scribe.

BELIEVE

Where are you?
Where are you now?
If not here, then where?
    Can I find you?
    Can I see you?
    Can I feel you?
Are you in my heart?
In my head?
Are you "on the other side"?
Can you even be found?
    Did you believe in Heaven
    and find your way there?
    But why? Oh why
    did you leave me, my child?
The day you died
I believed I might die, too.
But gradually something awakened
deep down inside of me,
and with the clarity that only
God can provide,
I knew I would find you.
    So, the seeker in me searched
    everywhere.
    In books, in classes,

in meditation and prayer
in dreams, and through tears.
So many tears.
I felt you draw nearer,
and I heard your voice
call out to me loudly,
with determination and force.
MOM!
At that moment
our new journey began.
I knew I could still have
a relationship
with you.
Over the years,
as my grief subsided
(just a bit),
I came to understand
the hows, the whys, and what ifs.
Not wanting me to waste the life I have left,
you helped me move
beyond the pain
of your death.
My heart still aches.
I will never let you go.
But I understand now it was all
part of our plan.

There is much work to do.
Our journey is never ending,
I know one thing for sure:
I found you!
You are here.
You are there.
You are everywhere.
You are the sun in my face
You are the wind at my back.
You are the trees swaying
You are the water cascading
You are young and happy and free!
You send me ladybugs and
oh, so many signs,
to remind me of
your never-ending love.
You give me hope.
You give me peace.
You give me understanding
and joy.
You give me all of this,
and so much more.
We hug!
We dance!
We laugh!
And sometimes, yes, we cry.

But I know you are with me
always,
loving me, guiding me,
always reminding me.
    A new relationship was born
    between us.
    Different, for sure,
    but still just as real!

        ~ ~ ~

What is death, my friend,
really?
Their bodies are gone,
but our loved ones are still here,

Because it's the Spirit
that never dies,
never leaves us behind.

So, open your grieving hearts,
open your minds
just a tiny bit,
and then
prepare to launch
a most fascinating ride!
You and your loved one,

together still.
Now and forever,
your relationship is real!

One heart, one love.
Healing and growing,
walking side by side
with gratitude
and in deep awe
of the miracle of life,
the miracle of Spirit!

Releasing our paradigms
about death and dying,
we come to understand
our true Purpose and true Self.

We come to know how blessed we are,
not in spite of our grief,
but because of what it can teach us!

For me, for you,
for all people who grieve,
we have just one word:
BELIEVE!

You CAN still have a relationship with your loved one. Just because you cannot see them or hear them does not mean that they aren't present. Can you hear or see gravity, yet do you believe? Can you hear or see the air that you breathe, yet do you believe? Can you hear or see your God, yet do you believe? Believe, my friend. Believe!

Chapter Twenty
Communicating with Your Loved One

As I said early on, I did find my son. And I learned how to communicate with him directly. It took time, a great deal of seeking, practice, and the decision to CHOOSE TO BELIEVE in order to do so. But I'm here to tell you my friend, if I did it then you can too.

There have been times when Bryan has spoken out loud, times when he has communicated through feelings in my body, times when he has communicated through the use of road signs, license plates, televisions, electronic devices, and meditation. One time I even saw a white mist swirling just below the ceiling of my closet, and I watched in amazement as it traveled up into the ceiling and disappeared. But much of my faith in the afterlife was always placed in the hands of mediums that I met along the way—other people outside of myself. I have had many readings with psychic mediums, some paid and many free. I have met extremely talented people who I know without a doubt are the real deal, and I have met some who clearly are not what they pretend to be. A couple of them are downright evil.

Let's talk about discernment for a moment. Discernment is critical, as I well learned the hard way! One time I was so desperate for information that I purchased a reading from a woman in Hawaii who advertised spiritual readings online. I didn't know this woman, nor did I know anyone who knew her. Yet I placed my heart in her unseen hands, and anxiously awaited my reading. What I received from her, in written form, shook me to my core. Basically, she told me (many times over) that I was not "of the light" and that my path was not "following the light." Can you imagine how distraught I was? I mean, virtually everything that I had explored and experimented with was of God, of God's light. Thankfully my intuitive friend Jill and psychic David Akins both refuted her statements and brought me out of my despair to where I could recognize how ridiculous and hateful her words were. I don't know what her end game was, maybe to pull me into some weird cult or something—who knows. But I do know that since then I have become very selective about whom I purchase spiritual readings from. As you pursue your journey into the unknown, it is so very important to use discernment and to always, always, always protect yourself with God's white light. While not common, it is possible for mischievous or mean spirits to try and thwart someone's spiritual awakening. I experienced something along those lines two different times in the early years of my awakening. For me, reciting The Lord's Prayer repeatedly drives such energies away and strengthens my protections that come from God's realm.

Back to communication and faith. So, while I truly believed in the signs Bryan sent us, the ladybugs and his other methods of reaching us, I remained a little bit doubtful about whether or not I could communicate with him *directly* without the help of a medium. Until one day, in the darkened hallways of a Portland hotel at midnight, a kind, extremely genuine and generous medium by the name of Roland Comtois pulled my friend and me over and told me that Bryan was present, and he had a message for me.

"He says, *'Keep looking, but don't go outside. Stay here [pointing to his heart]. No more mediums! You already know this. No more, you don't need another medium to say you didn't disappoint me, you didn't let me down. I've told you myself. You don't have to search any more, you don't have to search for me outside of yourself. I'm here, I'm here, I'm here!'"*

Roland continued, "You CAN talk to him, and he CAN respond to you. And I tell you—when it's absolutely him, versus your mind, it washes right over you. It's like a river of energy washing over you—you know it is true. When it's your mind, it comes and it goes, but when it's HIM it washes over you. And here's the thing: WHAT IF it was your imagination, and what if it makes you feel better? Because it could be your imagination once in a while. That moment of making you feel better gives you the courage to say it's true. Your boy says, *'No more mediums. No more asking, no more apologies.'* You've done well by your son. Everything that happened to your son was beyond your control. He loves you so. No more mediums. Just live as best you can, with him, loving him, connected to him."

I adore Roland Comtois. A medium, author, speaker, television and radio host, he channels spirit and travels internationally presenting his (free) signature "Purple Papers" which are eleven by seventeen purple papers where he records the spirit messages that he feels, hears and sees. I have been so very fortunate through my Sun Valley Moms group to have seen some of his presentations, and in fact I am the lucky recipient of four purple papers, three from Bryan and one from my dad.

Ever since Roland's generosity in delivering Bryan's message to me that evening in Portland, I have gradually learned to trust more and more. For me, direct communication with my son is telepathic. I hear him in my mind; sometimes I reply that way, but usually I reply out loud. If it's a particularly important or profound message from him (or anyone in spirit for that matter), I will experience a deep tingling up and down my entire body, which is how I know spiritual truth. Let me give you an astounding example of a telepathic communication I had with Bryan.

In 2015 I took an online course with Sue Frederick, who has

written numerous books including *Bridges to Heaven: True Stories of Loved Ones on the Other Side.* The course was an Intuitive Grief Coach training and certification, a very transformative training that teaches how to access intuition and connect to departed loved ones for guidance and healing—for yourself and others. After completion of the training I started practicing her techniques with friends whose children have passed on. The process involved my sitting in meditation prior to the readings, asking the children to be present and to share basic information with me, such as their sex, name, how they died, any validating information they'd like to share, etc. In the course of doing these readings, Bryan popped into one of my preparatory meditations. He said (telepathically), *"Mom, if you want we can do these readings for people for a business, and we can call it Love Letters From Heaven."* I chuckled and thought to myself, okay, fun possibility. But I never told a soul about it. Not even my husband.

Fast forward a year or so to a conference in Phoenix, Arizona where I was lucky enough to receive a free gallery reading from the amazing Susanne Wilson, The Carefree Medium. Susanne started out with generic information being given to her by a spirit, asking every audience member who connected to the information to please stand. Things like: I have a boy here, he is a young man in his early 20s, this boy loved to snowboard, he played sports, he was in the military, etc. As she continued, one by one people in the audience sat down until eventually I was the only person left standing. Susanne proceeded to give me one of the very best readings I've ever had. Virtually everything she said was accurate.

At the end of the reading, I was starting to sit when I heard her say "love letters from heaven." I straightened up and asked, "What did you say?" She repeated the phrase, and I was simply floored. I then told her about the significance of her words. This woman had repeated a phrase that my dead son had told me telepathically—a phrase that wouldn't have held meaning for anyone but me—a phrase that I had never written down nor repeated to anyone. How is this possible?

It's possible because it is real! If there was ever validation for Bryan working through me/with me/as me, this was it. This was HUGE validation for the greater reality that the soul never dies, and mind-boggling evidence of the work that Bryan is doing to remain a part of my life. I'm so grateful to him, and for him.

I talk to Bryan constantly, still, after almost twelve years since his passing. When I hear his reply, I don't doubt that it is Bryan. One of his favorite ways to notify me that he is present is to tousle my hair. Very frequently over the first five or six years after he died, I would be driving and I would experience the familiar feeling of someone tousling my hair. I could actually feel my hair moving, I could feel the tickle and tingle at my crown. He still does that sometimes, in the car and out of the car, and I just love it! I love the physical validations of his presence.

The experiences my healing journey have provided me have proven time and time again that it is real. HE is real. The afterlife is real. His name on that license plate is a message from him. That song on the radio is from him. That dream where he gave me the biggest hug was a real visit from him. The words and messages that pop into my head are from him. I feel his joy, his patience, his resolve—to not abandon me. I feel his love—unconditional, infinite, intense love. I feel his desire for me to be happy, and his absolute joy when I recognize all of these things to be true.

Maintaining communication between the worlds is as important to our loved ones as it is to us. And society historically hasn't wanted us to talk about it. We must change how we perceive the afterlife and our abilities to communicate with Spirit, and they with us. We must be okay with knowing that this current life is not all that we think it is—there is so much more to be discovered. I do think that the stigma attached to afterlife communication IS changing, and I believe it is becoming more accepted even within some religions. There is much ground-breaking research taking place, and who knows where it will lead. Afterlife communication as I learned it, and as I have attempted to present to you here, is not scary. It is not freakish. It is not bad, or wrong, or in defiance of God. It is OF GOD, it provides peace and comfort, it provides a pathway to healing our grief.

*L*et go of demanding proof that your loved one still exists. Trust that the voice you hear in your head is him. Trust that when you speak to her, she hears you. Honor them in this way; they are working hard to get through to you. Never forget that maintaining communication is as important to our loved ones as it is to us. Let them flood your consciousness and trust that it is truly them. Live your lives now with them at your side. Love is real, love is eternal.

Chapter Twenty-one
Love Is Eternal

I want to highlight an experience I had while participating in a group meditation at the Helping Parents Heal conference in Phoenix in the Spring of 2018. During the trance-like state that the meditation induced in me, I experienced the following:

My body was moving and swaying, and faces moved in and out of my awareness. I knew that the faces were spirits; there were so many of them, moving in and out of my vision. I went through a door into a meadow and I saw the most beautiful flowers—huge flowers like none I've seen on this earth. The colors were beyond my ability to describe, they were so vibrant. And the ladybugs! There were ladybugs of all colors and sizes, small ones on the flowers and large ones flying around the meadow. I was laughing and crying at the same time. I was so filled with anticipation—I knew my loved ones were near and I could barely contain my excitement. Back in the conference room, my physical body was still seated in its chair, tears streaming down my face. I crossed a bridge at the end of the meadow and instantly became aware of all of my loved ones. Bryan first, then my beloved dad and my beautiful mom, then all four of my grandparents. They began to send love to me, gently at first and then stronger, stronger, and stronger. They showered me with their unconditional love with such a force that it almost was painful to my physical body. As if they were one, they joined together and wrapped their love through me and around me—it became part of me. I have never felt such love before; I wish I could adequately describe to you the intensity and the power of it. Just when I didn't think I could hold any more, Bryan gently pulled me away. We were suddenly surrounded by a sky that was deep purple and there were dark clouds and specks of white (spirits) everywhere. I then saw that the sky was the ground and the ground was the sky, and yet above and around us it was just the Light. That beautiful Divine White Light. I realized then that Bryan was teaching me how he flies—he told me, "Remember the movement. There is freedom in the movement. It is this freedom that keeps me here—it's why I want to stay. My love for you is eternal." Then we floated some more before he turned to me one last time. We stretched out our hands and the tips of our fingers touched. Then my mom and dad were back with a personal message regarding my brother before they all faded away.

This was by far the most moving and powerful meditative experience I have ever had, and I've had quite a few good ones. My belief is that it wasn't just a meditation, this was a real visit from my son and loved ones. I believe that I was gifted a rare and glorious glimpse into the "Other Side" that day. I was shown a small part of the joyous reunion I will someday share with my son and my loved ones in Spirit. I cannot wait for that day, but while I am alive on this earth I have work to do. My son and I have work to do, together.

Remember my grandmother's words to me in that first dream visit, so many years ago? "It's okay darling, you will be with us soon." I didn't understand the meaning behind those words at the time. The teachers I studied with all taught that there is no "time" in the spirit world, at least not as we understand it. Thirty or forty years here is but a blip "over there." I know it may seem daunting to live the rest of your life on Earth without your beloved, but until it is our time to rejoin them, we owe it to ourselves, and to them, to live our lives as joyfully as we can, practicing love and kindness with every soul we encounter.

You have work to do, as well. Hold on to the belief that your loved one is not gone. He or she still lives, and you CAN still have a relationship. It is different, but it is oh so real! Don't give up. Hang on. Feel your way through your grief and become bigger than it is. Know that someday, you will have a most joyous reunion with your loved one. Until then, just believe. Believe!

Chapter Twenty-two
Grief Is a Journey

Grief is NOT a fast track, single lane highway that leads you immediately to a destination that might be labeled "BEYOND GRIEF." Oh no, my friends. Would that it be that simple, right? Rather, grief is a journey. A long, winding journey with many twists and turns, roadblocks, dead ends, alternate routes, and then, YES, wonderful destinations to eventually be reached. Those destinations, as we have expressed here, can include joy, peace, understanding, forgiveness, serenity, acceptance.

But the destination is not the prize here. The prize, if there were one, is the journey itself. It's all about the journey. How you choose to ride this twisted, heart-wrenching, gut-wrenching journey through grief will determine when, or sometimes if, you reach any of those destinations. Because, you see, you can't work your way around grief. You can't go under it or over it, you can't just move past it as quickly as possible. Well, you CAN, but you won't find healing that way. You'd only be bandaging your pain. In order to HEAL your grief and your pain, you must go THROUGH it. You must trudge through every sticky, muddy, painful, tearful part of it. It's about adapting to your new life without your beloved, or at least without your beloved in the form you are accustomed to. As Tom Zuba says, it's about learning to live life WITH the death of your loved one.

Let me explain.

Throughout my entire journey I have continued to study and learn life's important lessons—how to let go, how to accept, how to love, how to forgive. I learned new ways of thinking, new ways of healing, new ways of being.

I learned to recognize and appreciate all of the gifts that God and Bryan have given me in his death—the gifts of spirituality, self-love, deeper appreciation for all living things, respect for the choices a soul makes on his or her own unique life journey. I have learned to be present, to see with new eyes, to hear with new ears and to feel with a new heart. I have much more to learn, because I am far from a perfect human, but I will tell you this: I am a better person today than I was before my son died.

That's a big statement, to say I'm a better person today than I was before my son died. But it is absolutely true, and it doesn't shame me to admit it. And not only in some ways is my relationship with Bryan better today than it was before he died, but my relationships with other family members have strengthened as well. I know some of you reading this may have lost your only living child, as I did. And my heart breaks for you, for us. But I have to admit that I do feel blessed and fortunate to have "children of my heart"—my stepchildren—in my life, then and now. I love them so much and am so grateful they are part of my life. Steven and his fiancée and Jade, with one-month-old Tayler, came to the house every day for weeks after Bryan died. Kyle would join us after work for dinners and conversation. To this day we all go to the gravesite together on Bryan's birthday and celebrate his life. The kids and Dwaine all held their grief very quietly, privately, I think for fear that I couldn't handle their grief on top of my own. And they would have been right. As I have said, grief is selfish. I was so very selfish, but they never complained. They held me up and loved me, even when I couldn't show them that I loved them back. They asked for nothing from me, until that day many years later when, in frustration at long last, Dwaine reminded me that I wasn't the one who had died.

Remember when I told you that I had hosted psychic message circles at my home with David Akins just months after Bryan died? One of those was a private circle with our kids, some other family and a couple of close friends. I didn't know positively if Jade, Kyle, Steven and his fiancé, or my husband truly believed all of the experiences I was having. I knew they couldn't explain much of it, but sometimes belief in afterlife communication can be a big jump for people. I knew they were curious; I knew they wanted to believe, and I knew they would do anything they could to help me. After that message circle, the six of us remaining in our little family agreed upon a code word that we promised to tell a psychic medium if ever given the chance, after one of us transitioned into spirit, thereby ensuring that there would be no doubt.

My husband Dwaine was, and still is, my rock. My soulmate. The love of my life. He never questioned the path I took, the seeking I did or the time I spent away from him. Being the unselfish person that he is, he just wanted me to heal, to be happy again. I am so eternally grateful to him, now and always. And he loves and misses Bryan so much too, as does everyone in the family.

My sisters, brothers and father were also very supportive of me. Bryan was so loved within our family. He was the kind of kid who was always working to improve and challenge himself. He was smarter than all the rest of us, for sure. At an early age he was placed into the gifted and talented program in elementary school and received the Presidential Scholar Award when he was in the sixth grade. He was a 4.0 student, or close to it, throughout all of his school years. He won so many awards, I was always bragging about his most recent accomplishment to my friends and family. After he died I would just go to my dad's house and sit with him at his dining room table. We would just sit together—in pain, in silence. No words needed to be spoken. After I was Reiki certified, he would let me practice on his feet which caused him so much anguish from neuropathy. When I had a new tape recording from visiting David Akins, I would make my dad listen, and he would, even though he never really proclaimed a belief in any of it. In retrospect, I think all of that helped to prepare my dad for his own death four years later. During his dying days I overheard him talking to an invisible visitor (spirit) and he remarked out loud how proud he was of Bryan. Oh, how that warmed my heart!

Dwaine's family supported me as if I were one of their own. His sister Debbie mailed me a card *every week for a solid year* after his passing. Another sister and brother-in-law, Becky and Alan, traveled to Los Angeles with us to hold us up during the trial. All of their support meant so much to us, to me.

My relationship with Jere, Bryan's father, naturally grew distant. Because we shared Bryan when he was alive, we were in each other's lives and had occasion to communicate about affairs regarding our son. After Bryan's death and the trial, we didn't have a need to see each other. I did try to speak with him about the amazing spirit Bryan still was and the messages I was receiving, but he showed no interest in exploring further. I think he thinks I'm a little crazy, and that's okay. I had no choice but to let him live his life in peace. I do know that he is still married to Danetta, and they are happily enjoying retirement with their own grandchildren. He will always hold a special place in my heart.

I miss my son. I miss his slightly crooked smile that would light up his whole face and bring out a slight dimple in his left cheek. You couldn't help but smile back when you saw that smile. I miss his brilliantly blue eyes that twinkled all the time. I miss his laugh that was so sincere and joyous. I miss our conversations—sometimes we would only talk for a few minutes and sometimes it would be for an hour or more. We always said "I love you" at the end. I miss his constant teasing—he loved to push my buttons and make jokes at my expense, all good naturedly and in fun. I miss his humor—how he made me laugh! I miss that feeling of excitement every time Bryan would be coming home, cooking his favorite foods, cleaning his sheets, getting everything ready for his visit. Ever since Bryan left for college in 2003 a good part of my world revolved around when I would see him next. If he couldn't come home, we went to him. No sooner would we return from a visit with Bryan than I would be planning the next trip where I could see him again.

Those things are gone. But I can tell you without a doubt, I absolutely would not have survived losing my Bryan—Bryan in the physical, my son here on this earth—had I not found him in Spirit. Had I not heard his voice that day so very long ago—MOM!—which launched my spiritual awakening. With the absolute belief that there is life after death, belief that my son still lives, and belief that he is with me all the time, comes peace. For me, I can't imagine any other way. I am eternally grateful to him for continuing to be a part of my life.

As you progress on your own journey, you will have ups and downs; highs and lows. My hope is that you will continue on, never giving up. Seek out your own truths, your own understanding of why this tragedy has occurred in your life. You do not need to spend a lot of money or learn to be anything or anyone that you already are not. You are a spiritual being already, you just need to tap into that. Learn to know and trust your intuition, listen to the little voice inside your head. Become a seeker of your own truths.

Tell your story to all who will listen and allow yourself to feel all the pain and the anger that you hold inside. Let it out, don't be shy! Who cares what others might think? Make your own choices, honor yourself and your loved one in whatever way feels right to you. This is YOUR life, YOUR experience, YOUR healing.

Immerse yourself in everything that they were and still are— don't hide! Write down everything you can remember about them. Grieve, grieve, and grieve some more. Understand that you will heal, you will survive, if you so choose. Trust your inner voice and allow your own process to unfold.

Honor the flow of your healing journey. Don't compare your journey to another's. Only you know what is in your highest and best good. Try not to post angry comments on social media or engage in blame games. For example, the State of California sends us checks periodically that Bryan's killer earns for work he performs in prison, as part of the restitution that was awarded to us at trial. The checks range from a low of twenty dollars to a high of about seventy dollars. They used to arrive steadily every month, now it is much less often. We decided long ago not to keep the blood money. I used to post my outrage on Facebook every time a check would arrive. I would be incensed that I would be sent a twenty or thirty dollar check, as if that's what my son's life was worth! Then I started to just throw the checks away, in an effort to not be angry.

But Dwaine, who is such a kind and insightful man, suggested that we donate the money to a young girl we know who is in college, to help pay for her expenses. This is now our way of honoring the flow of events that were presented to us and trying to make good out of bad.

This book is my gift to you; I have presented to you my path, but you must follow your own path. Whatever that looks like for you, I ask you to consider making the choice to BELIEVE. Ask your loved one, "Where are you now?" and begin your journey toward finding them. Ask them for signs, signs and more signs. Seek to understand everything that you cannot see or hear. Open your eyes and your ears and your mind, be aware!

Choose to Believe. Choose Life. And when you're ready, learn to communicate with them. Set new goals for the life ahead of you and the new relationship you have with your loved one. Be the teacher. Pay it forward. You just never know who needs to hear what you have to say.

Choose to Believe.

Choose Life.

Choose Love.

Epilogue

This book was close to twelve years in the making. I started writing in the first year following Bryan's death, recording the detailed information which later formed the first three chapters. I always called it "my story" but intuitively I knew that the bigger story would someday be shared with others. In 2019 I got down to business. It became a pressing matter for me to complete the book, get it out to the world. So, I retired from my job and got to work. The words flowed (mostly) effortlessly out of me and onto paper. With the assistance of the most remarkable editor on the planet, friends, and beta readers, we fine-tuned each word, each sentence, each chapter. And then, just one week after I proudly announced on social media that my book was only one chapter away from being finished, I woke up with a condition called Adhesive Capsulitis, more commonly known as frozen shoulder. I couldn't lift my right arm more than a couple of inches without tremendous pain. I would be standing or walking and suddenly, with no warning, I would double over in pain. The pain traveled all the way down my arm, into my elbow, and oftentimes even further down into my wrist. I couldn't lift anything, or wash and dry my hair, or hang clothing in the closet, or reach upper cabinets to put dishes away. I couldn't lower my arm to the floor to tie my shoes, I couldn't weed my gardens or mow my lawn—and I most definitely couldn't write or type. I was practically paralyzed by the agonizing pain, twenty-four hours a day, seven days a week.

That ailment launched me on yet another intense journey of self-discovery and healing. I sought the help of a physical therapist who (not coincidentally) is also an amazingly talented energy worker. Together, we unfolded layer after layer of emotional pain that was buried incredibly deep inside of me. With each layer that we peeled back, there was more to explore and be revealed. At first the pain that unfolded was all about Bryan—deep pain and anger that I was still burying regarding his murder. And then the next session we would be pulled in deeper, and the next time deeper still. We "traveled" together every week over many months, she and I, and eventually the pain took us all the way back to when I was in my mother's womb. Back to when my pain began.

In the beginning I fiercely rebelled against this newly uncovered pain, professing loudly and many times over that I had done all the hard work already; I had done my inner child work years ago; I had grieved my babies and my beautiful son for so many years already. I screamed aloud that I didn't want to "go there" again, I didn't want to face the pain anymore. But the pain was relentless and, after months of fighting it and with Melanie's skill in helping me work with it, I came to relish the pain, and even to invite it in. I became curious—what would be revealed next? I visited my worst fears about my childhood and came to discover that they weren't real at all. I forgave my demons and embraced the little girl inside of me who was hiding, whimpering, looking for love. And one day, I just knew we were close to the end of the Chamber of Pain, as I had come to think of it. As if with new eyes, I was able to understand many things that had been beyond my grasp before the pain began. I saw and understood the ways in which I have enabled others, carried blame and responsibility for events and circumstances that were never my burden to bear. I saw ways in which I could be a better person: more empathetic, gentler, and kinder to everyone I meet.

I also intuitively understood that when the frozen shoulder left me, I would finish this book and it would be a better book than it would have been before, had I not experienced the frozen shoulder and all that the physical pain associated with it taught me. I saw the parallels between that physical pain, and the emotional pain of my grief. I saw that allowing the pain was necessary, critical even, to my healing. Just as it was in my grief healing journey.

I carried that pain for seven months. The work I did with Melanie eased the pain to the point where it was somewhat bearable, as did other treatments that I sought (massage and chiropractic adjustments). But although the pain was a little better, my mobility was not much improved at all. I was finally led to a local physician who performed a shoulder manipulation procedure in January 2020. From then on, my shoulder has improved each day, and I can now look back on the experience with clarity, rather than being stuck in it. I am able to see how the pain overtook me. My whole world was the pain, I became the pain. This, my friends, is what we have to do to heal. You never know how or when deeply-buried grief might manifest itself, and when it does, it is critical that we recognize and deal with it when it hits.

My friend and most amazing massage therapist Jean described it this way: "Think of each aspect of grief, each aspect of pain, as a string of thread in a strand of yarn. And all of those strings of thread unravel throughout the grief process. Imagine when you've allowed each of those pain emotions to come to the forefront and you've leaned into it, again and again, you've welcomed the pain of each thread. Then imagine all of those threads weaving into strands of yarn, and those strands of yarn are then woven together into the most beautiful sweater. The sweater is translucent, it's light, it's not at all constricting. It's soft on your skin, it's airy, it's so beautiful!"

The sweater is your story. How it will ultimately look and feel is entirely up to you. You are the master of your own creations. So create! Become the best version of you that you can be. There is so much inside of you still, waiting to be reborn, waiting to rejoice in a life that—believe it or not—still holds dreams and possibilities and adventures. As you walk through your grief healing journey, your loved one will be right beside you, helping to intricately weave your own beautiful sweater. You will wear it well; you will wear it proudly. After all, you did the work to create it!

APPENDIX:

THE SEEKER'S TOOLBOX

<u>BOOKS</u>

Eben Alexander, M.D., *Proof of Heaven*
George Anderson and Andrew Barone, *Lessons from the Light*
Ted Andrews, *Animal Speak*
Ted Andrews, *How to See and Read the Aura*
Vicky Bates, *Empty Jacket*
Ruth Berger, *They Don't See What I See*
Betty Bethards, *The Dream Book*
Master Choa Kok Sui, *Practical Psychic Self Defense for Home and Office*
Deepak Chopra, *Life After Death*
Aaron Christeaan, JP Van Hulle and M.C. Clark, *Michael, The Basic Teachings*
Ronelle Coburn, *Destiny at Your Fingerprints*
Roland Comtois, *16 Minutes*
Roland Comtois, *And Then There Was Heaven*
Roland Comtois, *Signs of Spirit*
Paul H. Dunn and Richard M. Eyre, *The Birth We Call Death*
Jill Renee Feeler, *Being Your Light*
Sue Frederick, *Bridges to Heaven*
Sue Frederick, *Your Divine Lens*
John Friedlander and Gloria Hemsher, *Basic Psychic Development*
Suzanne Giesemann, *Still Right Here*
Judy Hall, *The Encyclopedia of Crystals*
John Holland, *Power of the Soul*

Tanmaya Honervogt, *The Power of Reiki*

Mark Ireland, *Soul Shift*

John W. James and Russell Friedman, *The Grief Recovery Handbook*

Raymond A. Moody Jr., M.D., *Life After Life*

Chris Mulligan, *Afterlife Agreements, A Gift From Beyond*

Michael Newton, PhD, *Journey of Souls*

Michael Newton, PhD, *Destiny of Souls*

Brooke Noel and Pamela D. Blair, PhD, *I Wasn't Ready to Say Goodbye*

Jeffery Olsen, *Knowing*

Nick Ortner, *The Tapping Solution*

Sheri Perl, *Lost and Found*

Katrina Raphaell, *Crystal Healing*

James Redfield, *The Celestine Prophecy*

James Redfield, *The Celestine Vision*

Don Richard Riso and Russ Hudson, *The Wisdom of the Enneagram*

Colin Tipping, *Radical Forgiveness*

Eckhart Tolle, *New Earth: Awakening to Your Life's Purpose*

Brian L. Weiss, M.D., *Many Lives, Many Masters*

Suzanne J Wilson, *Soul Smart, 2nd Edition*

Wm. Paul Young, *The Shack*

Tom Zuba, *Permission to Mourn*

Tom Zuba, *Becoming Radiant*

GRIEF ORGANIZATIONS

Bereaved Parents of the USA *www.bereavedparentsusa.org*

Camp Widow *www.campwidow.org*

Grief Share *www.Griefshare.org*

Helping Parents Heal (Local Chapters and Semi-Annual Conference) *www.helpingparentsheal.org*

National Organization of Parents of Murdered Children, Inc. *www.pomc.com*

The Compassionate Friends *www.compassionatefriends.org*

The Grief Recovery Method *www.griefrecoverymethod.com*

The Grief Toolbox *www.thegrieftoolbox.com*

The Prayer Registry *www.sheriperl.com*

PSYCHIC MEDIUMS

Most of the following individuals offer private readings via telephone or online:

David Akins, Psychic/Medium, Reflexions Center
www.reflexionscenter.com

Roland Comtois, Spiritual Medium/Speaker
www.blessingsbyroland.com

Jill Renee Feeler, Intuitive Medium/Visionary
www.jillreneefeeler.com

Sue Frederick, Intuitive Coach/Speaker
www.careerintuitive.org

Suzanne Giesemann *www.suzannegiesemann.com*

John Holland *www.johnholland.com*

Laura Mirante, Spiritual Channel/Healer
www.lauramirante.com

Rachel Pearson, Spirit Messenger
www.rachelpearson.net

Tina Powers *www.tinapowers.com*

Susanne Wilson, Medium & Spiritual Teacher, The
Carefree Medium *www.carefreemedium.com*

ALTERNATIVE HEALING MODALITIES

Acupuncture—a widely known healing method, acupuncture may be used to help "open" the mind and body from an emotional perspective, but it can also be applied to physical symptoms of grief. *http://www.acupuncture.com/ newsletters/m_oct12/grief.htm*

Emotional Freedom Technique (EFT)—this very effective practice consists of tapping with your fingertips on specific meridian points while talking through traumatic memories and a wide range of emotions. *www.thetappingsolution.com*

Essential Oil Remedies—a remedy that can be very helpful with grief, stress relief, calming irritations, easing anxiety, improving overall mind and body health. Used topically or through inhaling by a diffuser, the essential oils can help aid the natural recovery and healing systems within your body and mind. Two well known oil providers are Bach Flower Essences *www.bachflowers.com* and Young Living Oils *www.youngliving.com*.

Massage—a therapy that can aid healing with touch. It is a powerful healing therapy that may remove stress and create harmony between our body, mind and soul. Massage has many benefits both physically and mentally for you. Not all massage is equal, explore massage therapists who are also attune to energetic healing. *www.massagewithjean.massagetherapy.com*

Integrative Physical Therapy—a therapy that focuses on identifying the cause behind the disease or dysfunction, not just soothing the symptoms. It can help us become aware of faulty postural, mental, emotional, or movement patterns that keep us from enjoying full health and wellness. Melanie Michaels with Mind, Body, Soul Physical Therapy provides such services. *https://www.mindbodysoulpt.com*

Pranic Healing—a non-touch energy healing modality developed by Master Choa Kok Sui. Prana means "energy" or "life force," and is also known as chi or ki. Prana is a necessary part of your "invisible" energy anatomy and is required for all physical bodily processes. *www.pranichealing.com*

Reiki—a healing technique based on the principle that the therapist can channel energy into the patient by means of touch, to activate the natural healing processes of the patient's body and restore physical and emotional well-being. *www.reiki.org*

CERTIFICATION PROGRAMS

Grief Recovery Specialist—the Grief Recovery Certification Training will give you the tools you need to effectively help grievers recover from loss as well as an opportunity for personal healing. *www.griefrecoverymethod.com*

Intuitive Grief Coaching—Sue Frederick offers both live online and pre-recorded workshops to be certified as an Intuitive Grief Coach. You'll learn sacred techniques for connecting to departed loved ones, and you'll master the Break Your Heart Wide Open meditation for healing and releasing grief. *www.careerintuitive.org*

Psychic Development—located in Nampa, Idaho, David Akins offers in-person psychic development workshops. Basic techniques, symbols and psychometry are learned in the beginning workshop and more advanced skills are taught in intermediate and advanced workshops. *www.reflexionscenter.com*

Spiritual Mediumship—Susanne Wilson offers an online pre-recorded multi-part series in spiritual mediumship suitable for anyone, including beginners. For advanced students she offers live online mentorship programs. *www.carefreemedium.com*

MORE TOOLS

Enneagram—a powerful and insightful tool to help us understand ourselves and others. The Enneagram helps us to see ourselves at a deeper, more objective level and can be of invaluable assistance on our path to self-knowledge. At a deeper level, the Enneagram tells us about the relationship between our personality and our Essence, or spirit. *www.enneagraminstitute.com*

HeartMath—helps to reduce stress and helps to bridge the intuitive connection between heart and mind, creating an emotional atmosphere for healing. *www.heartmath.com*

Journaling—starting a journal can help you manage your anger, your emotions and your grief. It also is wonderful for keeping track of your successes, your miracles and your dreams. A journal can be handwritten or typed. It can be in an expensive bound book or written on notebook paper. Writing can be very therapeutic.

Meditation—Wikipedia describes meditation as a practice where an individual uses a technique – such as mindfulness, or focusing the mind on a particular object, thought, or activity – to train attention and awareness, and achieve a mentally clear and emotionally calm and stable state. There are free and paid apps teaching all types of meditation techniques, such as Headspace, Calm, Insight Timer, Aura, Sattva, Inscape, and more.

Prayer & Gratitude—a powerful way to get out of yourself and re-center your being. Prayer is the act of deliberately communicating with your version of your God or Higher Power. Gratitude can help to make us nicer, more trusting, more social, and more appreciative.

Spirit Animals—spirit animals can show up in our awareness when the time is right, gifting to us a gentle reminder that we are connected to their divine energy and can call upon them to achieve our highest and best life. They can become teachers, guides and advisors when we most need it. www.*whatismyspiritanimal.com*

Walking & Hiking—a simple way to recharge, connect within and with nature to refresh the soul.

Yoga—works primarily with the energy in the body, through the science of pranayama, or energy-control. Prana means also 'breath.' Yoga teaches how, through breath-control, to still the mind and attain higher states of awareness. *www.ananda.org*

Acknowledgements

To my husband, Dwaine, thank you for always loving me and supporting this journey, even when you didn't understand it. You are my everything and I love you to the moon and back. My deepest love to Jade and Kyle Enzler, and Steven Lee and Anjuli Rodriguez for letting me love you as the children of my heart that you are.

For holding us up in our darkest days, I send deep gratitude to Lynn Perraud, Jill Ellsworth, Amy Blickenstaff, Darci Yarrington, and everyone in our large families who showed up in ways that were so special to us.

I send my forever and always love to Tayler, Ryenn, Maddyn, and Hadley for bringing me back to life, one hug at a time.

To Jess, Trevor, Tyson, Chris, Kamal, Rishab, Sadaf, Scott, Tanya, Luke, Mycolai, Zain, Gobind, Patrick, and Brandon: There are no goodbyes for us. Wherever you are, you will always be in our hearts. Frosty loved you all so.

I am beyond grateful to my editor, Dorothy Read, for your deep commitment to this book, and for your vision, encouragement and beautiful editing. You asked me to dig deeper, again and again. You believed in me before I believed in myself. Thank you to Pat Brunjes, Marilee

Petersen, Michele Coleman, and Faye Casebeer for reading and providing such valuable feedback on the manuscript, and to Lois Haynes and Grace Hansen for your eagle eye proofreading.

Tom Zuba, you have been a mentor and someone I have looked up to along this journey. Thank you, thank you, thank you, for honoring this book with your beautiful blessing; it means the world to me. Special thanks to Katie Mac for your superb camera skills.

And, to my dear friend Terry Hansen. Thank you for the beautiful custom design that so perfectly captured my vision, and which now graces the cover of this book. Thank you for your excellent interior design of its pages. Thank you for being with me, every step of this journey, and selflessly offering your amazing skills with all of my endeavors. Mostly though, I am grateful for all of our long hikes, weekends at the cabin in Stanley, and deep conversations about God and Spirituality. You encourage me to grow as a person.

ABOUT THE AUTHOR

Paige W. Lee is a dynamic Speaker, certified grief and transformation Coach, and Reiki practitioner. As a former Helping Parents Heal Affiliate Director, she now serves as a Caring Listener for the organization.

She lives with her husband, Dwaine, on a small acreage near Boise, Idaho, where she puts her passion for nature and gardening to good use. They love to travel and spend as much time as they can with their two remaining children and five grandchildren. She takes every opportunity to be outdoors and, especially, to hike the many trails in the spectacular hills and foothills near her home.

Choose to Believe is her first book, born of the pact she made with her son, after his death, to share their story and help others overcome the profound grief after the death of a loved one.

Made in the USA
Las Vegas, NV
20 February 2021